PEARLS
HOGS THE ROAD

Other *Pearls Before Swine* Books

Collections

Stephan's Web

I'm Only in This for Me

King of the Comics

Breaking Stephan

Rat's Wars

Unsportsmanlike Conduct

*Because Sometimes You Just Gotta Draw a
Cover with Your Left Hand*

Larry in Wonderland

When Pigs Fly

50,000,000 Pearls Fans Can't Be Wrong

The Saturday Evening Pearls

Macho Macho Animals

The Sopratos

Da Brudderhood of Zeeba Zeeba Eata

The Ratvolution Will Not Be Televised

Nighthogs

This Little Piggy Stayed Home

BLTs Taste So Darn Good

Treasuries

Pearls Gets Sacrificed

Pearls Falls Fast

Pearls Freaks the #*%# Out

Pearls Blows Up

Pearls Sells Out

The Crass Menagerie

Lions and Tigers and Crocs, Oh My!

Sgt. Piggy's Lonely Hearts Club Comic

Gift Books

Friends Should Know When They're Not Wanted

Da Crockydile Book o' Frendsheep

AMP! Comics for Kids

When Crocs Fly

Skip School, Fly to Space

The Croc Ate My Homework

Beginning Pearls

HOGS THE ROAD

A *Pearls Before Swine* TREASURY

STEPHAN PASTIS

Andrews McMeel Publishing®

a division of Andrews McMeel Universal

Dedication

**To Bill Watterson. What a thrill it was to work with you.
And
To Richard Thompson. What a thrill it was to know you.**

Introduction

This book contains 18 months' worth of *Pearls* strips. While I'd like to think that all of them are extraordinary (not true, but a guy can hope), three of them really *are* extraordinary. That is because they were drawn by *Calvin and Hobbes* creator Bill Watterson, who, in 2014, ended a 19-year hiatus from the comics page to draw three *Pearls Before Swine* strips.

For those of you who may not know the story, let me first reprint the blog entry I wrote at the time, and I will rejoin you at the end of it.

Ever Wished That *Calvin and Hobbes* Creator Bill Watterson Would Return to the Comics Page? Well, He Just Did.

Posted on June 7, 2014

Bill Watterson is the Bigfoot of cartooning.

He is legendary. He is reclusive. And, like Bigfoot, there is really only one photo of him in existence.

Few in the cartooning world have ever spoken to him. Even fewer have ever met him.

In fact, legend has it that when Steven Spielberg called to see if he wanted to make a movie, Bill wouldn't even take the call.

So it was with little hope of success that I set out to try and meet him last April.

I was traveling through Cleveland on a book tour, and I knew that he lived somewhere in the area. I also knew that he was working with *Washington Post* cartoonist Nick Galifianakis on a book about *Cul de Sac* cartoonist Richard Thompson's art.

So I took a shot and wrote to Nick. And Nick in turn wrote to Watterson.

And the meeting didn't happen.

Bill apparently had something to do. Or more likely, wanted nothing to do with me.

Which is smart.

But Nick encouraged me to send an e-mail to Bill anyways. I said I didn't want to bother him.

But a week or so later, this *Pearls* strip ran in the newspaper:

And I figured this was as good of a time to write to him as any.

So I e-mailed him the strip and thanked him for all his great work and the influence he'd had on me. And never expected to get a reply.

And what do you know, he wrote back.

Let me tell you. Just *getting* an e-mail from Bill Watterson is one of the most mind-blowing, surreal experiences I have ever had. *Bill Watterson really exists? And he sends e-mail? And he's communicating with me?*

But he was. And he had a great sense of humor about the strip I had done, and was very funny, and oh yeah . . .

. . . He had a comic strip idea he wanted to run by me.

Now if you had asked me the odds of Bill Watterson ever saying that line to me, I'd say it had about the same likelihood as Jimi Hendrix telling me he had a new guitar riff. And yes, I'm aware Hendrix is dead.

So I wrote back to Bill.

Dear Bill,

I will do whatever you want, including setting my hair on fire.

So he wrote back and explained his idea.

He said he knew that in my strip, I frequently make fun of my own art skills. And that he thought it would be funny to have me get hit on the head or something and suddenly be able to draw. Then he'd step in and draw my comic strip for a few days.

That's right.

The cartoonist who last drew Calvin and Hobbes riding their sled into history would return to the comics page.

To draw *Pearls Before Swine*.

What followed was a series of back-and-forth e-mails where we discussed what the strips would be about, and how we would do them. He was confident. I was frightened.

Frightened because it's one thing to write a strip read by millions of people. But it's another thing to propose an idea to Bill Watterson.

The idea I proposed was that instead of having me get hit on the head, I would pretend that *Pearls* was being drawn by a precocious second-grader who thought my art was crap. I named her "Libby," which I then shorted to "Lib." (Hint, hint: It's almost "Bill" backwards.)

At every point in the process, I feared I would say something wrong. And that Bill would disappear back into the ether. And that the whole thing would seem like a wisp of my imagination.

But it wasn't that way.

Throughout the process, Bill was funny and flexible and easy to work with.

Like at one point when I wanted to change a line of dialogue he wrote, I prefaced it by saying, "I feel like a street urchin telling Michelangelo that David's hands are too big." But he liked the change. And that alone was probably the greatest compliment I've ever received.

I don't want to say any more about our exchange because to do so would probably be to compromise the privacy he so zealously guards. But I will offer you this one biographical tidbit:

Technology is not his friend.

I found that out when it came to the logistics of the artwork. I drew my part first and then shipped him the strips. I wanted him to fill in the panels I left blank, and simply scan and e-mail me back the finished strips.

I asked him to do this because I did not want to be responsible for handling his finished artwork. Partly because I knew it would be worth thousands of dollars. Partly because I knew he wanted to auction it off for charity. And partly because my UPS driver has a tendency to leave my packages in the dirt at the end of our driveway. (I could just imagine the e-mail I'd have to write the next day: "Dear Mr. Watterson—The first comic strip you've drawn in 20 years was ravaged by a squirrel.")

So this left doing it my way. Digitally.

And this is when I found out that Bill Watterson is not comfortable with scanners or Photoshop or large e-mail attachments. In fact, by the end of the process, I was left with the distinct impression that he works in a log cabin lit by whale oil and hands his finished artwork to a man on a pony.

So I proposed working out our technological issues over the phone. But he didn't want to.

At first I thought it was because he didn't own one. Or have electricity. But then I remembered we were e-mailing.

And so I soon came to the sad realization that he probably just didn't want me to have his phone number. Which was smart. Because I would have called that man once a week for the rest of his life.

And so we worked through the technological problems via e-mail.

And unlike every other technological problem I've ever had, it was not frustrating.

It was the highlight of my career.

The only thing Bill ever asked of me was that I not reveal he had worked on *Pearls* until all three of his strips had run. [All these strips can be found on pages 52–53 of this book.]

And so I did not reveal his participation until now. And it was the hardest secret I've ever had to keep.

Because I knew I had seen something rare.

A glimpse of Bigfoot.

***

Okay, it's me in the present again.

Here to say that following the publication of this blog on June 7, 2014, the story exploded.

It was on the front page of the *Washington Post*, and was covered by CNN, ABC, NPR, NBC, *Rolling Stone*, *Time* magazine, the *New York Times*, and just about every other big newspaper in the United States, not to mention foreign publications from Australia to Ireland.

And the blog itself had 2,000,000 page views in one day.

It was, in short, the biggest story I've ever been a part of.

And the best part of all was that as the strips were running in newspapers, I got to meet the man himself. Because in the week the strips were being published, I just so happened to be in Washington, D.C., at the same time as Watterson.

We met at the home of the brilliant *Cul de Sac* cartoonist Richard Thompson. And for an hour or two, I got to ask Watterson everything I ever wanted to ask him. We talked about a whole bunch of different comic strips (*Peanuts* and *Doonesbury* and *Bloom County* and *The Far Side*, to name just a sampling), and we discussed comic strip timing and whether he regretted quitting and how he wrote the strip and where he wrote the strip and on and on and on until he was surely tired of me talking (and probably glad he never gave me his phone number).

And I want to tell you everything that I can remember about it. But . . .

. . . I'd feel really bad.

Because unlike me (who shares just about every embarrassing detail of my life I can think of), Bill really values his privacy.

So let me just say this: He no longer looks like he does in that one photo. (And really, whose 1985 photo looks good? Heck, I had a mullet.)

And at least a couple times, I made him laugh.

And that alone was the thrill of a lifetime.

Stephan Pastis
April, 2017

When I appear at book signings, I am often asked to draw Guard Duck, which is easy. But I am then sometimes asked to draw him with the rocket-propelled grenade launcher, which is much harder and would take about a half hour. So remember, if you come to a book signing, Stephan has limited skills.

My dentist does not know I draw a comic strip, so I can make fun of him as often as I want. He also doesn't know I only brush once a day, so don't say anything.

Ah, the killer whale. A character who has died, undied, died, and undied. Currently, I believe he is alive, but I am not sure. Whenever I'm unsure about something in the strip, I check Wikipedia, because whoever does the page for *Pearls* knows more about the strip than I do.

When I first started drawing the strip back in 2002, there was no way I could say the word "hell." Mostly because a lot of old people would have complained. But now, no one complains, which tells me that all of those old people have died.

14

OKAY, LITTLE WILLY, I'M HAPPY TO TAKE YOU TO THE FAIR, BUT THERE'S A LOT OF PEOPLE HERE, AND WE NEED A PLAN IN CASE WE GET SEPARATED.

NOW WHEN I WAS LITTLE AND MY MOM TOOK ME TO THE FAIR, SHE ALWAYS CARRIED A BRIGHT YELLOW BALLOON SO I COULD SEE HER ABOVE THE CROWD.

AND SHE WORE A BRIGHT RED SHIRT LIKE THIS, SO I COULD SEE HER EASIER.

BUT IF WE DO STILL GET SEPARATED, WE NEED A PLAN.

SO DO YOU SEE THAT BLUE TENT OVER THERE? THAT'S THE INFORMATION WINDOW.

IF ANYTHING HAPPENS, YOU RUN OVER THERE AND WAIT.

3/9

THEN I'LL NOTICE THAT YOU'RE GONE AND KNOW IMMEDIATELY WHERE TO FIND YOU.

DOES ALL THAT MAKE SENSE?

OR I COULD JUST CALL YOU.

TIMES HAVE CHANGED.

During my childhood in the 1970s, you actually had to make plans like this because nobody had cell phones. And as I write this, I suddenly feel like I am a 90-year-old man.

15

One time when I was in the checkout line at the grocery store, the checker asked me if I wanted to donate money for breast cancer. I said, "No, because I am against breast cancer," and left.

I got to swim once with a nurse shark in Mexico. Apparently, they are the most harmless breed of shark in the world. But to test that, I threw my son in the water first.

Even though I don't use the lemmings very much anymore, I liked the look of the cliff they always stood on and now use it for other characters.

I now own a swimming pool, which we heat with solar panels. But the solar panels are too powerful, so the water gets hot. It's not great for swimming, but it's terrific for boiling lobsters.

17

3/16

Little-known fact: If you ever read the Charles Schulz biography (*Schulz and Peanuts*) written by David Michaelis, I'm in it. In fact, I'm almost a page of it. It's because of an interaction I had with Schulz just a couple months before he died.

Panel 1: OKAY, GUYS, I HAVE AN IDEA. INSTEAD OF ALL BLINDLY JUMPING OFF THIS CLIFF LIKE THE LEMMINGS THAT WE ARE, WHAT IF INSTEAD WE EACH CHOOSE TO THINK FOR OURSELVES?

BUT THAT'S SCARY.

Panel 2: SURE, IT'S SCARY, PHIL. BUT THE ALTERNATIVE IS DEATH.

Panel 4: THAT'S DISCOURAGING.

My dim view of humanity in a nutshell. Except for you, the person reading this book. I like you.

Panel 1: WHAT ARE YOU DOING, PIG?

BUILDING STUFF WITH MY NEW ERECTOR SET. NORMALLY, I DON'T LIKE THESE THINGS 'CAUSE IT'S SO HARD TO DISASSEMBLE WHAT YOU BUILD, BUT THIS ONE AUTOMATICALLY BREAKS APART AFTER YOU'RE FINISHED.

Panel 2: IT'S THAT CONVENIENT?

YEAH. THOUGH IT DOES COME WITH A WARNING.

Panel 3: WHAT'S THE WARNING?

'SEE DOCTOR FOR ERECTOR BUILDINGS LASTING MORE THAN FOUR HOURS.'

Panel 4: PROUD OF YOURSELF?

HARDLY.

COMIC STRIP CENSOR

Panel 1: Hey, zeeba neighba...Want play croquet wid us and lemmings?

YOU'RE ACTUALLY PARTICIPATING IN RECREATIONAL SPORTS WITH OTHER SPECIES?

Panel 2: We use dem as balls.

Panel 3: BEATS JUMPING OFF CLIFFS.

I used to play croquet with my kids. But then I would lose and swear, so my wife took my mallet away from me.

19

Take a moment to examine that exquisite diagram of a person on the wall. It looks like Leonardo da Vinci's *Vitruvian Man*. Only better.

A speech balloon with a dotted line means that the character is whispering. Or that the artist is trying to save ink.

I actually know the guy who wrote *League of Denial* (Mark Fainaru-Wada), which is the story of how the NFL dealt with the concussion epidemic. (Side note: From time to time, you'll see me name-drop like that. It makes me feel important.)

When this series appeared, I got an e-mail from the office of Vince Gilligan, the creator of *Breaking Bad*. I sent him one of the strips from the series, and, in exchange, he sent me a whole bunch of cool shirts and magnets from the show. He also sent me the greatest handwritten note ever. It is based on a confession that Walter White makes to his wife about being a drug kingpin and a dangerous person to have at your front door ("I am the one who knocks!"). And thus, the note simply says, "Dear Stephan . . . YOU are the one who knocks!!!!" How he knew I was a drug kingpin, I'll never know.

As an added bonus, a couple days after I heard from Vince, I was at a book signing in Richmond, Virginia, when I was approached by Vince's mother, who wanted me to sign the *Breaking Bad* strips that were running that week in the newspaper. Finding out she was a fan of *Pearls* was very cool.

So the word that is deleted throughout this series is "methamphetamine." I don't know why, but mentioning a specific drug angers some editors.

Hey, I snuck the word "boob" in there. Not quite "methamphetamine," but I'll take it.

And speaking of deleting words, in what was a rather surprising development, the *Washington Post* refused to run this strip. And that was because it contained the word "midget." The ironic part was that the entire strip was about the Word Decider, a guy who decides which words you can use and which you can't.

You must always give the hand wave. If you learn nothing else from this book, let it be that.

Chuck D was a member of the hip-hop group Public Enemy. And if you're someone who believes in creationism, Charles Darwin was *the* public enemy. (And just like that, I show you how clever I can be, thereby justifying all the money you spent on this book.)

I do not have inappropriate magazines in the john.

I have never been friends with a guy who ties sweaters around his neck. I have standards. They're low, but they're there.

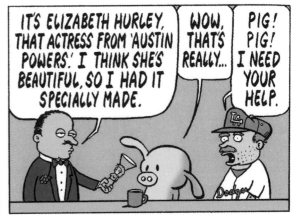

4/6

Probably the most popular strip of the year. And the only comic strip in history to contain a Mafia don, Elizabeth Hurley, and former Dodgers third baseman Ron Cey.

True fact: I once broke up with a girl on Valentine's Day. AND it was her birthday. You can boo me now if you'd like.

I once had one of my aunts proudly say to me, "I read your comic strip every day in the *Los Angeles Times*." Then she paused and added, "But I don't understand it."

NEWLY SINGLE STEPHAN TRIES PICKING UP WOMEN

I WANT TO TALK TO THAT WOMAN, BUT HOW? SHOULD I TELL HER WHO I AM? WHAT COMIC STRIP I DRAW? OFFER TO SKETCH HER SOMETHING?

PARDON ME, BUT ARE YOU STEPHAN PASTIS?

YES!! YES!! YOU RECOGNIZE ME! I'LL DRAW YOU SOMETHING! I'LL AUTOGRAPH SOMETHING! I'LL WRITE YOU SOMETHING!

UH... YOU DROPPED YOUR CREDIT CARD.

I'LL CRAWL INTO A HOLE.

Another true fact: I was in a restaurant last year in Montreal when I noticed a waitress taking her break and reading the newspaper comics section. I pointed to my strip and said, "I draw that one." She paused, looked up, and said, "So?" I never did that again.

NEWLY SINGLE STEPHAN TRIES PICKING UP WOMEN

I COULDN'T HELP BUT NOTICE YOU'RE READING THE COMICS PAGE... YOU KNOW, I DRAW A COMIC STRIP.

OH YEAH? WHICH ONE?

EVER HEARD OF 'CALVIN AND HOBBES'?

THAT WAS WRONG.

This was the comic strip I sent to Bill Watterson when I e-mailed him for the first time. (See the introduction on page 7 for the full story.)

RAT'S DECIDED HE'S NO LONGER GONNA MAKE DIRECT EYE CONTACT WITH OTHERS. HE SAYS IT MAKES HIM TOO NERVOUS.

HOW STUPID. DOESN'T HE HAVE A DATE TONIGHT?

YEAH, BUT HE SAYS HE CAN STILL BE A GREAT CONVERSATIONALIST.

THEY REALLY NEED TO RE-PAINT THIS WALL.

This is why it's best to just stay in the bar and drink.

The way you know that the man works at the Internal Revenue Service is that right above his desk is a sign that says "Internal Revenue Service." That's what is known in the business as "Cartooning Made Simple."

I showed a butt crack on the comics page. That's the kind of thing that makes me a pioneer of the medium.

I played with *Star Wars* figurines until I was 14 years old. And I didn't kiss a girl until I was 17. The two may be related.

"Is it wrong to Mace stupid people?" That's the kind of topic I'd like to see debated on NPR.

4/20

So if your kids ask you if the Easter Bunny is real, just show them this strip and say, "He was. Until he was beaten to death."

The iPhone has this feature where if someone calls you and you don't pick up, it sends you a prompt that indicates you missed a call. If you then swipe to open the phone, it automatically calls that person back. My friend Emilio did not know this and inadvertently called me eight times in a single week.

Judging by the poor drawing I did of that woman's anatomy, I'm not sure you'd want to look down her blouse.

I thought for sure I'd get a lot of complaints concerning the semi-sacrilegious nature of this one. But the complaints were minimal.

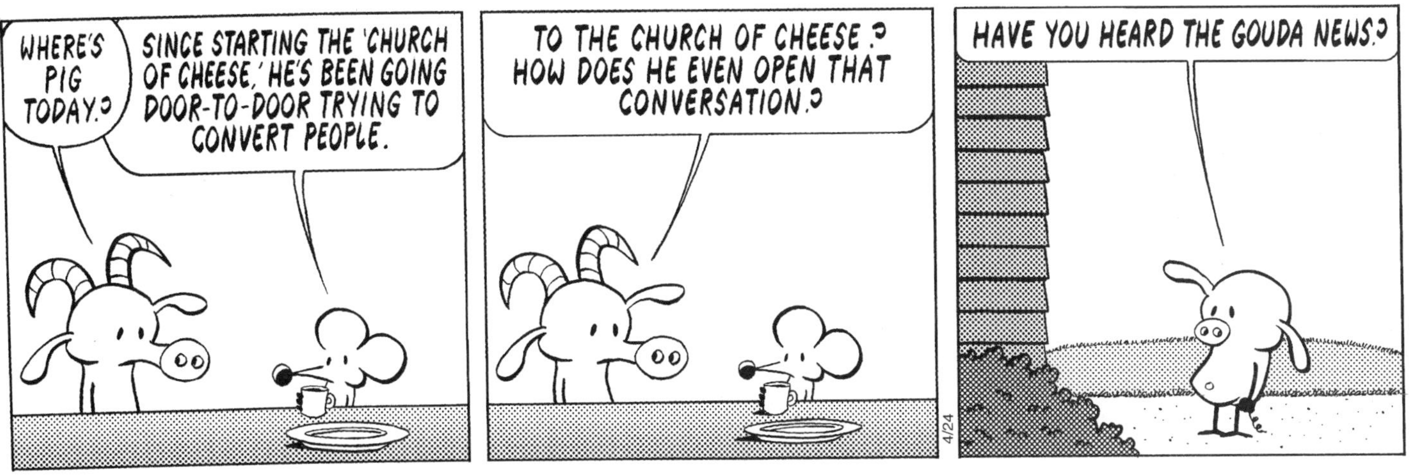
WHERE'S PIG TODAY?
SINCE STARTING THE 'CHURCH OF CHEESE,' HE'S BEEN GOING DOOR-TO-DOOR TRYING TO CONVERT PEOPLE.
TO THE CHURCH OF CHEESE? HOW DOES HE EVEN OPEN THAT CONVERSATION?
HAVE YOU HEARD THE GOUDA NEWS?
4/24

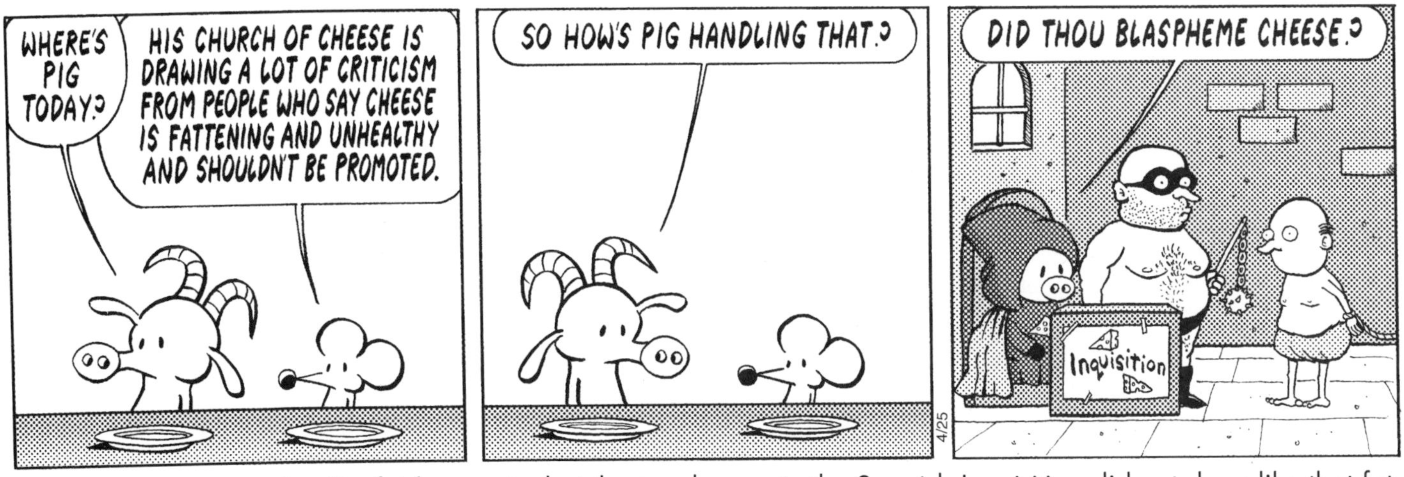
WHERE'S PIG TODAY?
HIS CHURCH OF CHEESE IS DRAWING A LOT OF CRITICISM FROM PEOPLE WHO SAY CHEESE IS FATTENING AND UNHEALTHY AND SHOULDN'T BE PROMOTED.
SO HOW'S PIG HANDLING THAT?
DID THOU BLASPHEME CHEESE?
Inquisition
4/25

I'm no history expert, but I'm fairly certain that the tough guys in the Spanish Inquisition did not dress like that fat guy in the middle.

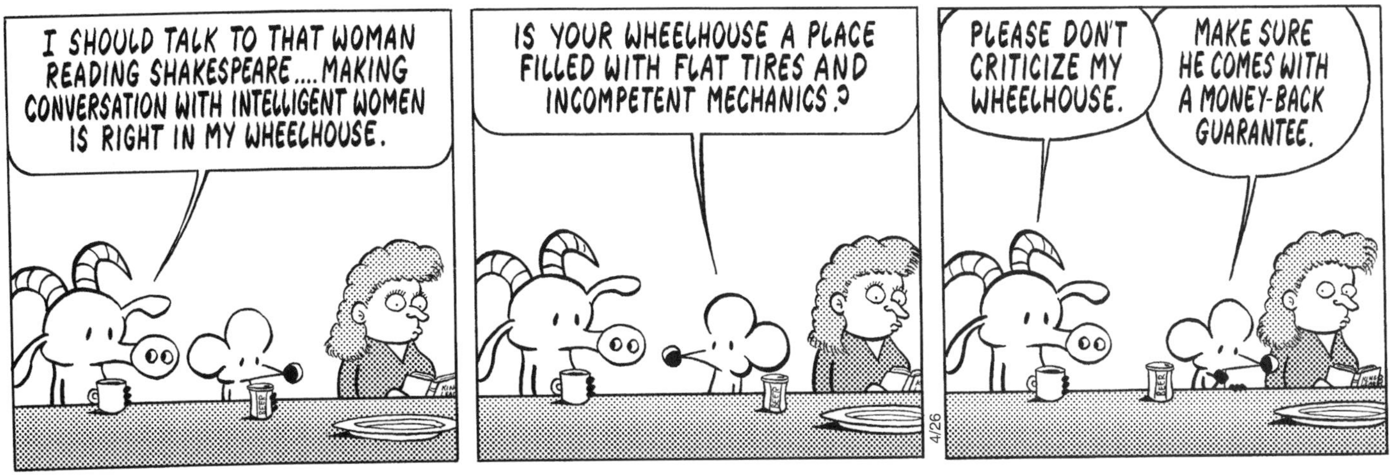
I SHOULD TALK TO THAT WOMAN READING SHAKESPEARE.... MAKING CONVERSATION WITH INTELLIGENT WOMEN IS RIGHT IN MY WHEELHOUSE.
IS YOUR WHEELHOUSE A PLACE FILLED WITH FLAT TIRES AND INCOMPETENT MECHANICS?
PLEASE DON'T CRITICIZE MY WHEELHOUSE.
MAKE SURE HE COMES WITH A MONEY-BACK GUARANTEE.
4/26

Presumably, Jack then burns to death and dies. Spoiler alert.

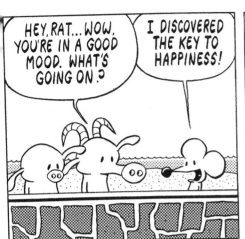

Aww. This one's just sad. Maybe that will be my new mission. To just make you sad.

While I can draw some dogs (like poodles), I cannot for the life of me draw a collie. But only "collie" rhymes with "dolly," and thus I was screwed.

I didn't know if I could get away with so clearly telegraphing the word "ass" in that last panel. But I did it anyway. And the world as we know it did not end.

5/4

Some people really do get cryogenically frozen in the hope that one day they can be revived. I would do it, but I hate to be cold.

Apparently, it's "Preserve Dead Things Forever" week in *Pearls Before Swine*.

Rat looks very strange to me whenever he smiles or laughs. Unless it's a maniacal laugh. Then it's in character.

I probably shouldn't tell you this. But if you go to the last panel, and look at the last word in Pig's speech balloon, and then look to the right of it at the first word in Rat's balloon, well, you'll see how juvenile I really am.

I will only buy toilet paper at the grocery store if I'm buying a whole bunch of other stuff with it. Otherwise, it looks like I made a special trip to the grocery store just for toilet paper. And that feels wrong.

I CAN'T BELIEVE THAT LITTLE MOSQUITO HAS BEEN ENCASED IN THAT AMBER FOR SIXTY MILLION YEARS.

IT'S STRANGE, HUH?

YEAH. AND HE'S BEEN TOTALLY PRESERVED.

THAT'S TRUE. PROBABLY DOESN'T LOOK MUCH DIFFERENT THAN HE WAS THEN.

SO BEING FOSSILIZED LIKE THAT IN TREE RESIN IS A BIT LIKE BEING IMMORTALIZED. YOU'RE PRETTY MUCH GUARANTEED TO BE AROUND FOREVER.

ONE STEP AHEAD OF YOU.

YOU CAN'T BREATHE IN RESIN.

WHO CARES ABOUT BREATHING WHEN YOU CAN BE IMMORTAL?

WOULD IT BE WRONG TO GO THROUGH HIS WALLET?

Rat shouldn't be able to breathe, see, talk, or be heard in that amber. Mostly because he'd be dead. So if you're citing this strip in support of your doctoral thesis in biology, there may be issues.

After this series ran, *Wheel of Fortune* sent me a cool photograph of Vanna White and Pat Sajak standing by a puzzle that reads, "WHEEL LOVES PEARLS BEFORE SWINE." So there—at least somebody loves me.

There were some *B.C.* strips that had Christian themes. So I thought who better to pair those characters with than a foul-mouthed drunk?

43

I somehow managed to make Vanna White look like a bug-eyed alien freak. But never mind that—my Andy Capp is brilliant.

My son now goes to the same university that I did. So whenever I drive him back to school, I slow down in front of my old apartment building and say, "What famous cartoonist once lived in that building from 1988 to 1990?" And he always answers, "Jim Davis?" He really gets on my nerves.

IF ABRAHAM LINCOLN HAD TWEETED....
— An Alternative History —

Take that, you little troll, Stephen Douglas.

THE GETTYSBURG ADDRESS

 Follow

Abraham Lincoln
@Honest_Abe

87 yrs ago, our fathers did stuff. Now big war. Govt by people good.

ON THE SOUTH'S FIRING UPON FORT SUMTER

Follow

 Abraham Lincoln
@Honest_Abe

OH NO YOU DI'INT

THE EMANCIPATION PROCLAMATION

 Follow

Abraham Lincoln
@Honest_Abe

Slaves free! (if living in Confed.) Rest of you - not so much. #DoingBestICan

5/18

FORD'S THEATRE

Follow

 Abraham Lincoln
@Honest_Abe

Play s'posed 2 B good. Am dying to see.

PLEASE DON'T WRITE ABRAHAM LINCOLN TWEETS.

IT'S LIKE I'M CHANNELING THE GUY.

DID HE ENJOY THE PLAY?

Strange fact about Stephan: I am, for reasons I can't justify, inexplicably drawn to places where famous people were killed. So far I've been to Ford's Theatre (Abraham Lincoln); Dealey Plaza (John F. Kennedy); the Lorraine Motel (Martin Luther King, Jr.); the Dakota (John Lennon); and a home in Jackson, Mississippi (Medgar Evers).

WHAT ARE YOU DOING, PIG?

PLAYING WITH MY VIKING ACTION FIGURINES. THEY'RE ABOUT TO BATTLE.

OOOH...VIKING COMBAT...I LIKE THAT...WHAT DO THEY USE? SPEARS? SWORDS? BATTLE AXES?

Q-TIPS.

AT WORST, THEY'LL GET CLEAN EARS.

Apparently, you're no longer supposed to use Q-tips to clean your ears. I don't know why that's true, or *if* it's true. But I do know this: If you're taking health tips from me, you've got bigger problems than Q-tips.

DO YOU THINK COMIC STRIP CENSORSHIP IS MORE STRICT THAN THE CENSORSHIP YOU SEE IN OTHER FORMS OF MASS ENTERTAINMENT?

DOES A BEAR SIT IN THE WOODS?

CURSE YOU, TRICKY RAT.

WHAT NOW?

NO MORE TALK OF BEARS IN THE WOODS.

DO YOU THINK OUR CREATOR, STEPHAN, HAS BEEN ACTING A LITTLE LESS MATURE LATELY?

WHAT MAKES YOU SAY THAT?

I'M IN MY CHOO CHOO JAMMIES.

THERE'S THAT.

HA HA. STEPHAN LIKE CHOO CHOO JAMMIES.

It's been years since I owned "choo choo jammies." And when I say "years," I mean last year.

I have never owned a cool sports car. Unless you count my four-door Honda Accord. Which is fly. Or dope. Or whatever expression the youngsters are using today.

Do any of you really think I live in a basket on the front porch of my house? If so, it's not true. I live on the *back* porch.

This really is sort of how corporations work.

This was based on a brewery in Minnesota that developed and used a drone delivery system.

And the government really did stop them. Stupid government. You'd think the one thing they could protect would be the beer-delivering drones.

This strip is *almost* sweet. Until all that talk about murder.

I actually started doing this with my kids. But I swore so much that we lost track of the total.

Hey, that really looks like a wagging tail. Or a breadstick.

And thus begins the week of strips I worked on with *Calvin and Hobbes* creator Bill Watterson.

I called the little girl "Libby" because it then gets shortened to "Lib," which backwards is "Bil." Which is not quite how Bill spells his name. But hey, there are no little girls named "LLib."

I loved seeing Bill's version of Rat and Pig. It was so much different than my own.

This strip and the prior two were auctioned off and raised a total of over $74,000 for Parkinson's research.

Libby's line in the second panel ("There's a magical world out there to explore") is the final thought expressed by Calvin in the very last *Calvin and Hobbes* strip. So this was yet another clue that the guest artist was Bill Watterson.

53

For those of you who might not know, I write a middle-grade series called *Timmy Failure,* the fifth volume of which came out in 2016. That little boy in the sixth panel is supposed to be Timmy.

I don't mind when they pass around the donation basket at my church. But what I do mind is that it forces me to interact with other people, most of whom annoy me. Which perhaps means that the church's fundamental message of brotherly love is not getting through to me.

This really is true. If you ever go on the internet to try to look up what your symptoms mean, you'll find you're going blind and have a fatal disease and are at that very moment having a stroke.

55

HEY, RAT, THIS IS MY FRIEND, BARNEY BARNACLE. I WAS TALKING TO HIM ABOUT POLITICS, BUT HE DOESN'T EVEN KNOW WHO BARACK OBAMA IS.

WHAT—HAVE YOU BEEN LIVING UNDER A ROCK?

THAT HURTS.

My daughter and I sometimes go to the beach and climb over the rocks at low tide, where we find all kinds of sea creatures. So far she hasn't been washed out to sea, so it's been a positive experience.

WELL, RAT, MY GIRLFRIEND PIGITA AND I ARE OFF TO THE BIG SACK RACE AT THE PARK.

YOU GUYS ARE GOOD AT THAT?

OH, SHE'S GREAT IN THE SACK.

YOU NEVER KNOW WHAT'S GONNA SET HER OFF.

My dad told me that he liked this strip. I think it's one of only four or five strips he's ever mentioned to me.

HOW COME IF YOU LOOK AT PHOTOS OF PEOPLE FROM THE 1800s, ALMOST NOBODY IS EVER SMILING?

WELL, PIG, THAT'S A COMPLEX QUESTION, BUT I SUPPOSE IT'S BECAUSE—

THEY HAD NO SUPER BOWL, NETFLIX, OR CHEESE PUFFS.

OF COURSE.

NO, NOT 'OF COURSE.'

THERE WAS NO HAPPINESS BEFORE THAT.

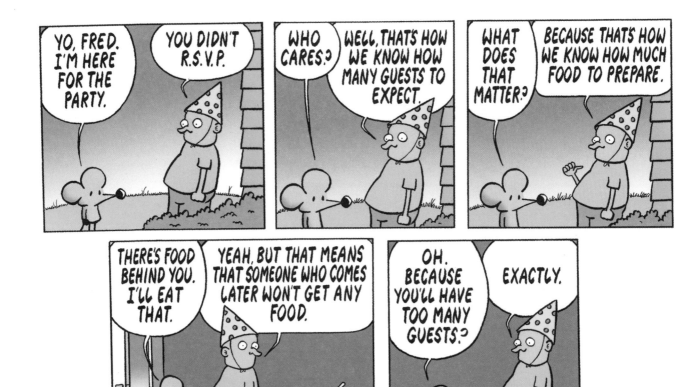

Why did I have Rat go for the fruit salad? He would have grabbed as many beers as he could carry and walked out the back door.

For future generations reading this book: Joe Biden was the vice president of the United States. (As if future generations will read this book.) (Or even read.) (Or be alive.) (Wow, this just gets darker and darker.) (And this is the longest line of parentheticals ever.)

I wanted to make this guy a regular character, but it took too long to draw the chainsaw. So I stopped.

This was funny in my head. Then it got onto paper.

Compounding the problem, I brought him back the next day.

This really did appeal to a very narrow audience. Give yourself five *Pearls* points if you knew both Richie Rich *and* the song reference. (By the way, *Pearls* points are redeemable for nothing. Unless you want to go out and get a beer that you pay for yourself. You can do that with your *Pearls* points.)

This joke is so dumb that I would ask that you all just turn the page and hope for better.

For those of you who might not know, that's Dilbert's boss in the last panel. *Dilbert* is a comic strip. A comic strip is a series of sequential panels designed to make you laugh.

Whenever I fail to follow the path that the GPS lays out for me, the woman's voice says, "Recalculating." But she says it with attitude, as if what she's really saying is, "Hey, dumbsh#t, can't you follow directions?"

Rare, serious note: It's really absurd that we keep an animal as awesome as the elephant in captivity so we can force him to do tricks for us. I think future generations are going to look at that the same way we now look at 19th-century "freak shows." Just stupid and cruel.

WHAT ARE YOU DOING, GOAT?

PROTESTING THE CIRCUS THAT'S COMING TO TOWN. I DON'T LIKE THEIR TREATMENT OF ANIMALS.

FREE THE ELEPHANTS

OH, THAT'S A GREAT CAUSE. HOW LONG HAVE YOU BEEN OUT HERE?...

ALL DAY. NOW I'M HUNGRY. WHAT ARE YOU EATING?

FREE THE ELEPHANTS

FREE THE ELEPHANTS

NEVER EAT CIRCUS ANIMAL COOKIES AT A CIRCUS ANIMAL PROTEST.

But it's okay to eat circus animal cookies. Because as far as I know, they're not made from real circus animals. Unless somewhere there are very tiny elephants coated in sugar.

I DON'T GET IT. I KEEP BUYING THINGS TO TRY AND MAKE MYSELF HAPPY, BUT NONE OF IT MAKES ME HAPPY.

WHAT DOES THAT TELL YOU?

I'M BUYING THE WRONG THINGS.

NO.

I NEED BETTER, MORE EXPENSIVE THINGS!!

DO PEOPLE IN CHINA READ MYSTERY NOVELS?

WHY WOULDN'T THEY?

WELL, I THOUGHT THEY READ BOOKS FROM BACK TO FRONT.

YEAH. SO?

SO THEY'D ALWAYS SPOIL THE ENDING.

IT'S QUIET TIME NOW.

I liked this joke. Sometimes I think I am really talented.

SPARE A MINUTE?

YOU'RE THE ENCYCLOPEDIA SALESMAN. GONNA TRY TO SELL ME SOMETHING ELSE THAT THE INTERNET NOW GIVES ME FOR FREE?

NOPE. THIS TIME I'M JUST COMING TO YOUR DOOR FOR A HANDOUT.

WHY SHOULD I GIVE YOU A HANDOUT?

BECAUSE THE INTERNET'S DESTROYED EVERYTHING—RECORDED MUSIC, CABLE T.V., NEWSPAPERS, MAGAZINES, ENCYCLOPEDIAS...ALL BECAUSE YOU AND YOUR WHOLE GENERATION EXPECT ALL CONTENT FOR FREE.

SO?

SO IT'S NOT FREE. IT'S PRODUCED BY FICTION WRITERS, NEWS REPORTERS, ROCK MUSICIANS...AND IF THINGS DON'T CHANGE, WE'RE ALL GONNA BE KNOCKING ON YOUR DOOR.

WHATEVER, OLD MAN.

KNOCK KNOCK KNOCK

SPARE A MINUTE?

I was sort of hoping I'd hear from KISS guitarist Paul Stanley after this ran. But I did not. Maybe he was too busy going door to door.

Why does the side of every single house in *Pearls* look the same? I'll tell you why. Laziness.

Don't try this at home.

I was sort of surprised I could get away with Rat's line in the last panel because it so clearly telegraphs the word "ass." To mitigate its impact (and thus the potential complaints), I ran it on the Fourth of July, figuring that less people read the strip on holidays.

While at a restaurant near the University of Arizona, I met a student whose father was a mortician. She explained how her dad drained the blood from dead bodies, all while I sat there and ate an enchilada. It was a bad time to eat an enchilada.

If I die an untimely death, or even a timely one, and you all decide to create the Stephan Pastis Memorial Museum, I want the gift shop to offer the Cooked-Squid-on-Roller-Skates-Clock-Radio.

(1) Raisins aren't that big; (2) they don't have eyes; (3) they don't have arms and legs; and (4) they rarely talk. Other than that, this strip is pretty realistic.

Tip O' the Day: Every year or so, my wife calls the cable company and tells them we want to cancel cable, and in response, the cable company either lowers our bill or gives us something for free. So please, everyone go out and do that.

WHAT ARE YOU LOOKING AT ON YOUR PHONE, GOAT?

THESE PHOTOS OF A TEMPLE IN EGYPT. THAT SEMICIRCULAR RECESS IN THE BUILDING IS CALLED AN APSE.

WHAT'S PAINTED ON IT?

THOSE ARE THE SNAKES THAT ARE SAID TO HAVE KILLED CLEOPATRA.

WOW. AND YOU FOUND ALL OF THIS ON YOUR PHONE?

YEAH. ON THESE APSE ASPS APPS.

TRY SAYING IT THREE TIMES FAST.

TRY WRITING A JOKE THAT'S NOT LAME.

7/9

HEY! MY OLD FRIEND, TOM! I HAVEN'T SEEN YOU IN YEARS. HOW GOES IT?

OH, CAN'T COMPLAIN. I'M STILL MARRIED. I HAVE TWO WONDERFUL KIDS.

I THOUGHT YOU HAD THREE.

PICK PICK PICK PICK

7/10

TWO THAT ARE WONDERFUL.

Below is the original image of that kid, as I submitted it to the syndicate.
See if you can find what detail the syndicate eliminated.

PICK
PICK PICK
PICK

I've been traveling to England a fair amount over the past few years and I never know whether to say "football" or "soccer." Because if I go to a pub and say "football," they'll assume that because I'm American, I mean the game that has quarterbacks and touchdowns. But if I say "soccer," they'll think to themselves, "Stupid American." So now I just go to the pub and drink quietly.

Danny Donkey got lectured by his friends.

YOU DRINK TOO MUCH, DANNY DONKEY.

BAD DANNY.

Beer isn't good for you, Danny Donkey.

You can't live your life inside a bottle, Danny.

So Danny defied his friends and slipped inside a bottle.

Where he enjoyed the smell.

Beer smells nice.

BE

And the beer goggle view.

YOU'RE ALL SO PRETTY.

7/13

And the muffled sound.

Nirvana achieved, Danny never came out of the bottle again.

URP.

POSITIVELY UPLIFTING.

SOME LECTURES BACKFIRE.

WAIT FOR ME, DANNY DONKEY!!

So for the record, while a kid cannot drink a beer in *Pearls*, an angry donkey can. That seems somehow racist.

WHAT ARE YOU DOING, DAD?

Me got take written driving test, but ees pretty easy.

You have been in a collision with a parked vehicle and can't find the owner. You must:

Escape widout beeing seen.

Duh.

And stupid crocodiles can drink beer, too. But what if that was Junior's beer there? Ooh, now there's an ethical dilemma.

LARRY TAKES HIS WRITTEN DRIVING TEST

There is no crosswalk and you notice a pedestrian crossing in front of you. You should:

HIT WID CAR TO TEECH LESSON.

You acing dis.

WHAT ARE YOU DOING, PIG?

I'M STUDYING ALL THE WORLD'S RELIGIONS AND PHILOSOPHIES AND TAKING NOTES ON WHAT SEEMS TO BE THE TRUE ROAD TO HAPPINESS.

WHAT DO YOU HAVE SO FAR?

I like pizza.

IT MAY BE THE KEY.

I'm gonna publicly admit right now that my favorite pizza is that Hawaiian one covered in pineapples and ham. And please don't tell me that you like anchovies or olives. We will not be able to be friends.

Rest assured that if one day you become a syndicated cartoonist and decide to depict a nun being kicked in the rear, you will get e-mails that look like this:

Mr. Stephan Pastis,

I noted in the cartoon run on July 18, 2014, the "joke" of the strip is kicking a nun. Now I was educated by nuns. While there were times that they found me a challenge, these women were always held in highest esteem. This cartoon in my estimation is tasteless and disrespectful. Please, consider the object you humor before targeting this esteemed group.

And here's another e-mail I received:

I thought the previous day's strip that made fun of nuns was unique. I was wrong. A friend told me you had an earlier one in which a sister administered an enema. I would like to know why you target Catholics.

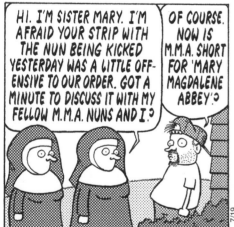

And yet not one person complained about a cartoonist being kneed in the groin. Oh, the double standard.

This came from calling my dad on my iPhone. I have two numbers in there for him: one labeled "home" and one labeled "cell." So to specify, I'd always have to say, "Call Dad home," like I was God telling him his time was up.

Being a California boy, I have never in my life seen an actual armadillo. Though I hear they die a lot.

That loofah looks more like the trunk of an elephant who is lying on his back on the other side of the wall. I may be the only cartoonist in recorded history who managed to make a loofah look like an elephant.

WHERE YOU OFF TO, GOAT?

MY SPIN CLASS.

YOU NEED A CLASS TO LEARN HOW TO SPIN?

THEY DON'T TEACH US HOW TO SPIN. WE RIDE BIKES.

TO WHERE?

NOWHERE.

HAHAHAHA HAHAHAHA HAHAHAHA HAHAHAHA HAHAHAHA

OKAY, NOW BE SERIOUS.

I like people who park as close as possible to the gym so they don't have to walk a long way. Then they go inside and walk on the treadmill for an hour.

MY FRIENDS INVITED ME TO THEIR PLACE OF WORSHIP, BUT I'M NOT GONNA GO.

WHY NOT?

THEY HAVE RABIES.

RABIES?

HIS FRIENDS ARE JEWISH. AND THE WORD HE'S LOOKING FOR IS 'RABBIS.'

WE SHOULD HAVE THESE DISCUSSIONS LESS OFTEN.

My syndicate did not want to run this because they thought that Jewish people would be offended. Their argument was that I was comparing "rabbis" to "rabies," which I thought was a little ridiculous. They ultimately agreed to run it. And if there were complaints, I didn't hear of any.

HI, RAT. IT'S YOUR MOTHER. I'M CALLING TO TELL YOU THAT AUNT MILLIE DIED. HER MEMORIAL'S ON TUESDAY. HER FUNERAL'S ON WEDNESDAY. AND INSTEAD OF SENDING FLOWERS, THE FAMILY WOULD LIKE PEOPLE TO MAKE DONATIONS TO SAINT ANTHONY'S, HER CHURCH ON MAIN STREET.

YOU'RE QUIET. DO YOU NEED A MOMENT?

YES. TO FIGURE OUT WHO AUNT MILLIE IS.

I'M NOT AS CLOSE TO MY FAMILY AS I COULD BE.

I don't know why, but when I write the *Timmy Failure* books, I do this every morning. I sit down to write at 8 a.m., and yet I don't actually start writing until about 11 a.m. Do all writers do that? Or am I just special?

And so begins a Very Special Week of *Pearls Before Swine.*

As I think I've said before, using the Comic Strip Censor Guy lets me get away with a lot of stuff I otherwise couldn't get away with. Because no editor wants to risk looking like him.

77

This is the difference between my strip and a strip like *Baby Blues*. In *Baby Blues*, the main characters are human, and so if the mother is depicted drinking beer while pregnant, the creators of the strip are deluged with complaints. But since my characters are animals (and therefore more in the fantasy realm), I get fewer complaints about something like this.

I don't have one witty thing to say about this strip. But I felt the need to fill this space anyway.

Stephan strolls down memory lane.

WHEN I was a KID, MY DAD drove me AROUND IN THE back OF his PICKUP truck.

BOUNCE BOUNCE

WHEN I WAS a KID, I FLEW ACROSS the COUNTRY by mySELF.

WHEEEE

WHEN I was A Kid, I spent EVERY summer DAY in my friend's SWIMMING POOL And HIS parents were rarely HOME.

WOOHOO

WHEN I was a KID, I ate EVERYTHING I dropped on THE GROUND AND some STUFF THAT was ALREADY thERE.

MMMM... GUM.

WHEN I was A kid, every INJURY I got was TREATED WITH a PAT on the HEAD And a 'WALK IT off.'

Hmmm

8/3

Stephan babysits his nephew in 2014.

HERE'S HIS LIST OF ALLERGIES, SOME GAMES THAT IMPROVE HIS COGNITIVE SKILLS, AND PLEASE STAY WITHIN 18 INCHES OF HIM AT ALL TIMES.

I DON'T KNOW WHETHER TO FEEL SORRY FOR YOU OR ME.

LET'S GO CRAZY AND EAT TRANS FATS.

Panels 2, 3, and 4 are straight out of my own childhood (the pickup truck, the flight, the pool). In fact, I can remember one of my childhood birthday parties where my dad put me and ten of my classmates in the back of a pickup truck and drove us all to get pizza. We all survived.

WELL, DOCTOR, IS IT A BOY? A GIRL?

IT'S NOT A GIRL.

IT'S A BOY! IT'S A BOY!

IT'S NOT A BOY.

I'M VERY CONFUSED.

WE ALL ARE!!

When we looked at the ultrasound for our second child, I told the doctor that it looked like an elephant. She ignored me and wrote down the sex of the baby and sealed it inside an envelope (because we told her we wanted it to be a surprise). But on the way to the car, my wife and I decided we just couldn't wait to find out the sex, so we tore open the envelope. It said, "It's a girl! Not an elephant."

RAT'S ULTRASOUND

DOCTOR, IF I'M NOT HAVING A BOY OR A GIRL, WHAT'S IN MY BELLY?

LASAGNA. YOU ATE TOO MUCH LASAGNA.

LASAGNA? THAT CAN'T BE. I MEAN, I DID GO TO GARFIELD'S HOUSE, AND WE DID HAVE LASAGNA, BUT THAT CAN'T BE ALL LASAGNA IN THERE.

IT'S NOT.

OH, THIS IS AN UPLIFTING SERIES.

JIM DAVIS'S LAWYER ON LINE THREE.

I CAN'T BELIEVE I ATE GARFIELD. THAT'S BAD, ISN'T IT?

YEAH. JIM DAVIS IS GONNA BE PRETTY UPSET. YOU SHOULD GO TO HIM AND APOLOGIZE.

ISN'T HE, LIKE, THE HEAD OF THE WHOLE GARFIELD EMPIRE?

HE'S A CARTOONIST LIKE ANY OTHER CARTOONIST. JUST GO AND SEE HIM.

A VISITOR APPROACHES, MY LORD.

OFF WITH HIS HEAD.

THE CAT SEES ALL

In the gap between when I wrote this series and when it appeared in newspapers, I actually visited Jim Davis at his studio in Indiana. Because I didn't want him to think the series was a commentary on my visit, I had to alert both him and his large staff that this series was upcoming. I must say that it is not easy to stand in the literal center of the *Garfield* universe and announce that Garfield gets eaten and killed.

Jim's studio really is in the middle of nowhere. If he wanted to, he could give directions by simply saying, "Drive to our town, and when you see a building, that's us."

For some reason, Jim Davis's doctor really liked this strip. So at Jim's request, I sent his doctor a signed print of it. When Jim thanked me for sending it, he added, "Your car is in the mail."

8/10

I hesitated a bit to do this strip because I knew that certain people would see it as a commentary on the Affordable Care Act (i.e., Obamacare), which it wasn't. I just thought it was a good opportunity to show the crocs doing something stupid. It's amazing how people now are just *waiting* for an opportunity to yell at each other over any political issue they can find.

I like mocking the notion that strips have to have a certain continuity to them. *Pearls* has none. Things happen, and then they unhappen.

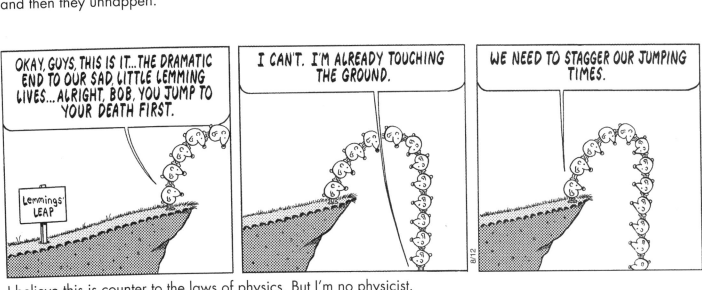

I believe this is counter to the laws of physics. But I'm no physicist.

Doofi. And just like that, I've invented a word.

If I am not mistaken, I believe a fan suggested this joke to me. I get a lot of ideas sent to me (tons, in fact), but in 15 years of doing the strip, I think I've only used five or six of them.

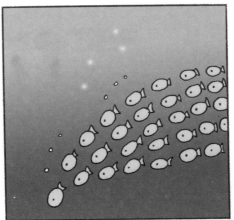

8/17

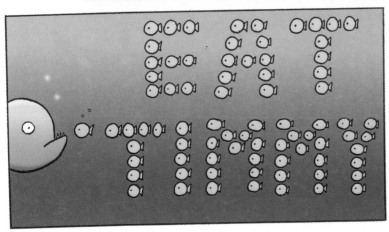

In *Pearls*, the name "Timmy" is code for "character who will die soon."

I really do keep meticulous track of every book I've read. I've done it for years. And after this strip appeared, I heard from a lot of people who do the exact same thing.

I often eat alone (mostly because I'm alone so often on book tours). And sometimes when the host takes me to a table, they remove all the extra glasses and silverware with extra gusto, as though announcing to the room, "Loser here can't find anyone to go to dinner with him."

I'm tempted to make Pilly Wonka a regular character. I like both his name and the concept of him throwing around pills instead of candy.

Safety warning insisted upon by my publisher, Andrews McMeel: Don't put children in ovens. Not even the annoying ones.

That quote at the beginning of the strip is an actual quote from the U.S. Supreme Court's decision in a case called *McCutcheon v. FEC*. And if you think that's true, and that money does not corrupt the system, try making an appointment to see your senator tomorrow. It won't happen. But it will if you donate a million dollars. There is an easy solution to this: public financing of elections. Nobody running for office could take a single dollar from a donor, and we could once again have a representative government.

I'LL SEE YOU LATER, RAT. I HAVE TO FLY WITH THESE MINERS TO THEIR MINING CONVENTION.

WHY DO YOU HAVE TO DO THAT?

AIRLINE RULES.

WHAT AIRLINE RULES?

NO UNACCOMPANIED MINERS.

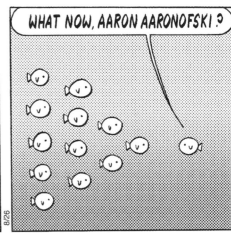

DO YOU REALLY MAKE A LIVING FROM THIS?

HEY CHIEF...WE ALWAYS SWIM IN SCHOOLS, HOPING THAT THE OTHER GUY GETS EATEN, BUT HOW 'BOUT SOMETHING MORE ORGANIZED, LIKE DYING ALPHABETICALLY?

MAKES SENSE TO ME. ANYONE OPPOSED?

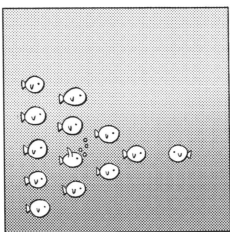

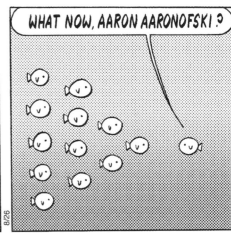

WHAT NOW, AARON AARONOFSKI?

This strip really made me laugh. But I'm not sure it made a lot of other people laugh. I think the disconnect was that many people didn't see that one fish in the second panel raising his fin to ask a question.

RAT WENT TO McDONALD'S CORPORATE HEADQUARTERS.

WHAT FOR?

HE'S TIRED OF ALL THEIR OLD CHARACTERS, LIKE RONALD McDONALD AND GRIMACE AND MAYOR McCHEESE, SO HE WANTS TO PITCH A NEW ONE TO THEM.

WELL, THAT'S NICE. WHO'S THE CHARACTER?

I THINK WE'LL PASS ON 'MR. McWHISKEY BARREL.'

When I was a little kid, my grandmother took me to McDonald's once a week. Because she was a child of the Great Depression, she always saved every extra napkin and ketchup packet and took them home.

89

RAT PITCHES NEW CHARACTERS TO McDONALD'S

SIR, WE APPRECIATE YOUR PITCHING NEW CHARACTERS TO US, BUT WE'RE HAPPY WITH THE ONES WE'VE GOT.

BUT YOU NEED AN ANTAGONIST.

YES, WELL, WE AT McDONALD'S HAVE THE HAMBURGLAR FOR THAT, SO I THINK WE'LL PASS ON... ON... ...WHAT'S HIS NAME AGAIN?

MR. McPUNCH-YOU-IN-THE-FACE.

RIGHT.

I wonder sometimes if the executives at McDonald's have a sense of humor about strips like this, or if they even read them. Unlike other companies I've mentioned (such as Home Depot, General Mills, and Sierra Nevada Brewing), I've never heard from anyone at McDonald's. Maybe that's a good thing.

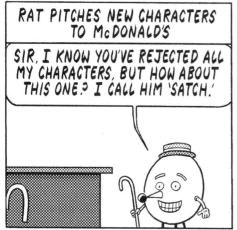

RAT PITCHES NEW CHARACTERS TO McDONALD'S

SIR, I KNOW YOU'VE REJECTED ALL MY CHARACTERS, BUT HOW ABOUT THIS ONE? I CALL HIM 'SATCH.'

SATCH, HUH? KINDA CUTE. IS IT SHORT FOR SOMETHING?

SATURATED FAT MOLECULE.

SECURITY, PLEASE.

LOOK, KIDS! I CLOG YOUR VEINS.

But if the good folk at McDonald's *are* reading these strips, I'd like to suggest that they make Satch the Saturated Fat Molecule a new character.

HEY, GOAT, WANT SOME OF MY CHILI CHEESE FRIES?

I THOUGHT YOU WERE SUPPOSED TO BE ON SOME NEW DIET WHERE YOU BURN OFF MORE CALORIES THAN YOU TAKE IN.

I WALKED TO THE KITCHEN TO GET THEM.

I'D GO BACK FOR A MILKSHAKE, BUT I'M TOO WINDED.

8/31

Pig's line in the last panel ("Fly me to Candyland!") is a reference to the Sunday strip just before this one (where the congressman flies away on a unicorn).

HEY, RAT... DO YOU HAVE TO OPEN A NEW BAG OF CHIPS? THERE ARE THREE OPEN ONES IN THE CUPBOARD.

YEAH, BUT THERE'S BARELY ANYTHING IN THEM.

THEN WHY DON'T YOU JUST THROW THEM OUT?

BECAUSE AS A GENIUS, I MUST GUARD MY TIME ZEALOUSLY.

THAT GETS HIM OUT OF A LOT OF THINGS.

Another strip that is straight out of my actual life. I never eat the last chip or nut or cookie, because that would necessitate throwing out the package. And I am much too lazy for that. And ladies, if that doesn't make me an attractive catch, I don't know what does.

HEY THERE, GOAT... I'D LIKE YOU TO MEET MY FRIEND WALLY THE WALRUS. HE JUST GOT A TEACHING JOB.

OH, YEAH? TEACHING WHAT?

AEROBICS CLASSES.

THEY'RE SHORT CLASSES.

I'M AFRAID I OFFENDED THE WHOLE L.G.B.T. COMMUNITY.

YOU? WHAT DID YOU DO?

I DIDN'T USE GREASY ENOUGH BACON ON MY BACON, LETTUCE AND TOMATO SANDWICH.

WHY WOULD THEY CARE ABOUT THAT?

WHAT ELSE WOULD THE LETTUCE GREASY BACON TOMATO COMMUNITY CARE ABOUT?

PLEASE MAKE IT STOP.

Nobody from the LGBT community complained. Neither did anyone from the BLT community.

A lot of people really do think that expressing gratitude is the key to happiness. I think the key is to drink beer all day on the beach. But I am grateful that I have beer. So maybe they're on to something.

Another joke that seemed funny in my head. I can find myself very amusing in there.

HEY, GOAT. WHATCHA DOING?

PRACTICING MY SINGING. I'VE BEEN TAKING VOICE LESSONS.

GOOD. HOW'S IT GOING?

OKAY, EXCEPT FOR THE HIGH NOTES. I DON'T KNOW WHY, BUT THE TREBLE RANGE IS HARD FOR ME.

YOU REALLY STRUGGLE WITH IT?

YEAH. SO MUCH SO THAT WHEN I SING IT, I SCRUNCH UP MY FACE, GIVING IT THIS DEEP, FURROWY LOOK...OR AT LEAST THAT'S WHAT MY VOICE TEACHER TOLD ME YESTERDAY.

WHAT ARE YOU GUYS TALKING ABOUT?

9/7

YESTERDAY, ALL MY TREBLES SEEMED SO FURROWY.

GOD, I HATE THIS COMIC STRIP.

LET IT BE.

I recently did a book tour that took me through Liverpool. While there, I got to see the childhood homes of both Lennon and McCartney, as well as Penny Lane and Strawberry Fields. I also took this photo by the grave of Eleanor Rigby.

This strip is sort of a continuation of the Sunday strip a few pages back.

Note: 'Hi and Lois' co-creator Brian Walker recently called Stephan Pastis and asked if he'd like to guest-write a 'Hi and Lois' strip. Stephan has agreed.*

Brian Walker, one of the current creators of *Hi and Lois*, wrote me an e-mail on the day this appeared, stating simply, "These things happen in the best of families."

After this strip appeared, the *Des Moines Register* ran a short article about it titled, "*Pearls Before Swine* Goes Iowan." So remember, kids, butt-kissing really does work.

I am allergic to cats. I know that's not particularly interesting, but I couldn't think of anything else to say here.

Whenever my kids tell me how lame or stupid I'm being, I remind them that my entire genetic code is in every single cell of their body. Then they get depressed.

After this strip appeared, a physicist wrote to me to say that Physicist Phil "is eerily accurate."

HEY, PHYSICIST PHIL, HOW GOES IT?

GOOD. I'M DOING A PEER REVIEW OF A FELLOW PHYSICIST'S SCIENTIFIC PAPER.

OH, WONDERFUL. WHAT HAVE YOU WRITTEN SO FAR?

My colleague is a fathead poopypants.

IT'S GOTTEN PERSONAL.

There was a time when my syndicate would not let me say the word "poop." But those days are over. Victory is mine.

WHY IS THE PLACE THEY PUT YOUR COMIC IN THE NEWSPAPER CALLED THE 'FUNNY PAGES'?

BECAUSE THE WORK I DO IS MEANT TO BE FUNNY.

IS THERE A 'SAD, BUT DOING HIS BEST' PAGE?

THIS SEEMS TO BE A SENSITIVE SUBJECT.

True fact: Unlike almost every other cartoonist (most of whom use a tilted drawing table), I really do work on a flat desk. Behold:

In the early years of the strip, when I still looked at internet message boards, I found a comment by an old college roommate of mine talking about the strip. He said how stupid he thought it was. But I thought he was stupid. So I think that makes us even.

9/21

I don't have anything specific to say about this strip. So here are some blank lines for you to fill in your own commentary:

HEY, FATHER GUS, HOW DOES THE CHURCH DECIDE WHO GETS TO BECOME A SAINT?

IT'S A COMPLICATED PROCESS. WHY DO YOU ASK?

BECAUSE I LET A WOMAN BUYING ONE ITEM CUT IN FRONT OF ME IN THE GROCERY STORE LINE.

I DON'T THINK THAT'S ENOUGH.

I RECYCLED A BEER BOTTLE ONCE.

I didn't find your last comments that witty. Have another try: _____

_____

I HEARD YOU'RE SUBMITTING AN APPLICATION TO BECOME A SAINT. WHAT COULD THAT POSSIBLY BE BASED ON?

I LET A WOMAN WITH ONE ITEM GO AHEAD OF ME IN THE GROCERY STORE LINE.

WAIT A MINUTE. I WAS THERE THAT DAY. YOU SAID YOU DID IT BECAUSE SHE WAS HOT AND YOU WERE HOPING THAT SHE'D TALK TO YOU.

HAVE SOME MONEY FROM THE CHURCH BASKET.

SAINTS DON'T BRIBE.

(Whoa. This is a big time-saver. Here, just keep doing it yourself.) _____

WHERE'S PIG TODAY?

SOME MOM HIRED HIM TO DO FACE PAINTING AT HER SON'S BIRTHDAY PARTY.

OH, KIDS LOVE THAT. HAS HE DONE IT BEFORE?

NO. WHY?

I THINK YOU MISUNDERSTOOD.

My book editor tells me that she does not find this "blank line" thing amusing. She says no more blank lines.

Okay, I'm back. Here to say that we have seven neighbors around our property. We like five of them and dislike two of them. So from that I conclude that I dislike 2/7 of humanity, or 28.5 percent.

9/28

I see a brilliant, handsome, cartooning stud.

104

So if you had the choice to know how you were one day going to die, but you had no ability to prevent it, would you still want to know? I would. Because I'd go around telling everybody exactly how I was one day gonna die, and when it happened I'd look like a prophet.

If we get to find out everything we've always wanted to know when we die and go to heaven, my first two questions are gonna be: (1) who killed John Kennedy; and (2) why was printer ink so expensive?

An older lawyer in my law firm told me that he always attended the funerals of other lawyers that he hated. When I asked him why, he said, "Because I wanted to be sure the sons of b#tches were really dead."

This really is why filing cabinets only let you open one drawer at a time. Because otherwise, people would be crushed by filing cabinets. On the list of noble ways to die, that one would not rank high.

10/5

My wife and I auctioned off the original of this strip for charity. To keep an eye out for such auctions and everything else *Pearls* related (including ways to get signed books), just go to the *Pearls* page on Facebook: facebook.com/pearlscomic.

Do you see a secret message hidden in the typed text in Panel 2?

And do you see a secret message hidden in the typed text in this strip? See answers below in next comment.

ANSWERS: There are no hidden messages. So if you saw one, you should be concerned.

Every year for various holidays, I draw cards for my wife and kids. Then I color them in with crayons. I do this for two reasons: (1) I like coloring; and (2) I'm too cheap to buy real cards.

No blind people complained about this strip. Then again, they couldn't see it.

Around one out of every two new characters in the strip is named Bob. There are two reasons for that: (1) It's a short word, so it fits easily into the speech balloons; and (2) the word just sounds funny to me.

A company really did ask me to do a strip that would be beamed to Mars, and thus I drew this strip. As far as I know, no Martians laughed.

I've never carpooled to work. But it does remind me of the time I was in high school and a fellow student gave me a ride to a speech tournament. Apparently, I was rather obnoxious during the drive, because at one point she stopped the car on the side of the freeway and told me I had to walk the rest of the way.

Every time I do a book signing, someone in the audience will ask if I'm really divorced. And no, I am not. Nor does my wife feed me out of a dog bowl.

I really had just read a huge biography of Van Gogh at the time I drew this strip. It was called *Van Gogh: The Life.* I was fascinated by the ending where the authors explain that Van Gogh may not have killed himself. Instead, some of the evidence indicates that he may have been shot by a little kid.

This was by far and away the most popular strip of the year.

When I was a lawyer, my office was right next to another lawyer who kept all of his documents in incredibly neat piles on his desk, with each side of the piles perfectly parallel to the edges of his desk. So every time he left, I would turn the piles a few degrees to the right or left. It drove him insane.

My wife has never tried to donate me to The Salvation Army. Though at times she has wanted to.

Rat is me here. I truly do not get the oyster thing.

Now mayonnaise. There's a food I enjoy.

There are two things you'll see a lot of in *Pearls*: (1) beer, which Rat is usually drinking; and (2) boxes. I am truly obsessed with putting characters in boxes. Stupid people, pushy people, stupid crocodiles—I've put them all in boxes. Where do these twin obsessions come from? Well, look how I spent my childhood:

And here in the very next strip is beer. All this strip needs now is a box.

You don't see a lot of stoned chickens on the comics page. Except in *Pearls*. No wonder my mother's so proud of me.

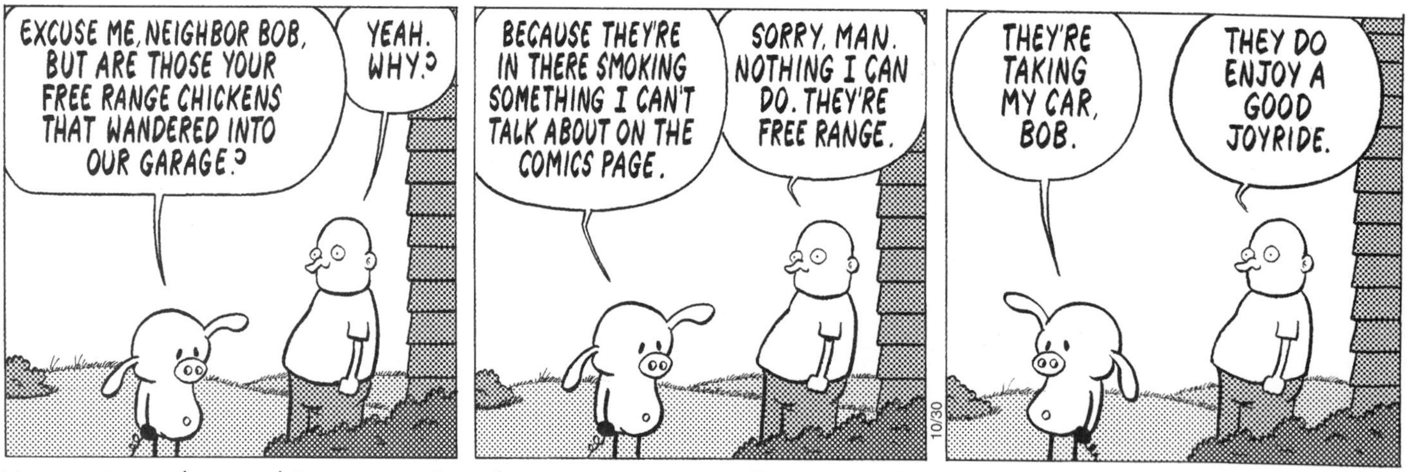
EXCUSE ME, NEIGHBOR BOB, BUT ARE THOSE YOUR FREE RANGE CHICKENS THAT WANDERED INTO OUR GARAGE?
YEAH. WHY?
BECAUSE THEY'RE IN THERE SMOKING SOMETHING I CAN'T TALK ABOUT ON THE COMICS PAGE.
SORRY, MAN. NOTHING I CAN DO. THEY'RE FREE RANGE.
THEY'RE TAKING MY CAR, BOB.
THEY DO ENJOY A GOOD JOYRIDE.
10/30

You can't say the word "marijuana" on the comics page. Well, you can, but you're guaranteed to get letters. And not the kind that say you're a wonderful cartoonist.

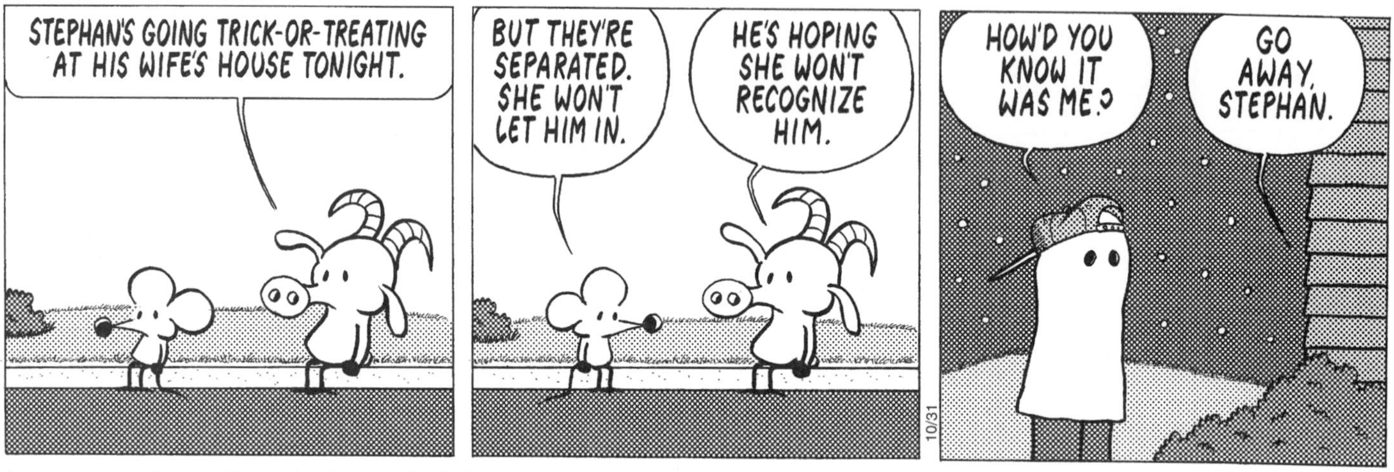
STEPHAN'S GOING TRICK-OR-TREATING AT HIS WIFE'S HOUSE TONIGHT.
BUT THEY'RE SEPARATED. SHE WON'T LET HIM IN.
HE'S HOPING SHE WON'T RECOGNIZE HIM.
HOW'D YOU KNOW IT WAS ME?
GO AWAY, STEPHAN.
10/31

A rare strip that acknowledges a holiday, in this case Halloween. Because I'm generally seven months ahead of deadline, I don't reference too many holidays. It's just too hard to think of Christmas gags in May.

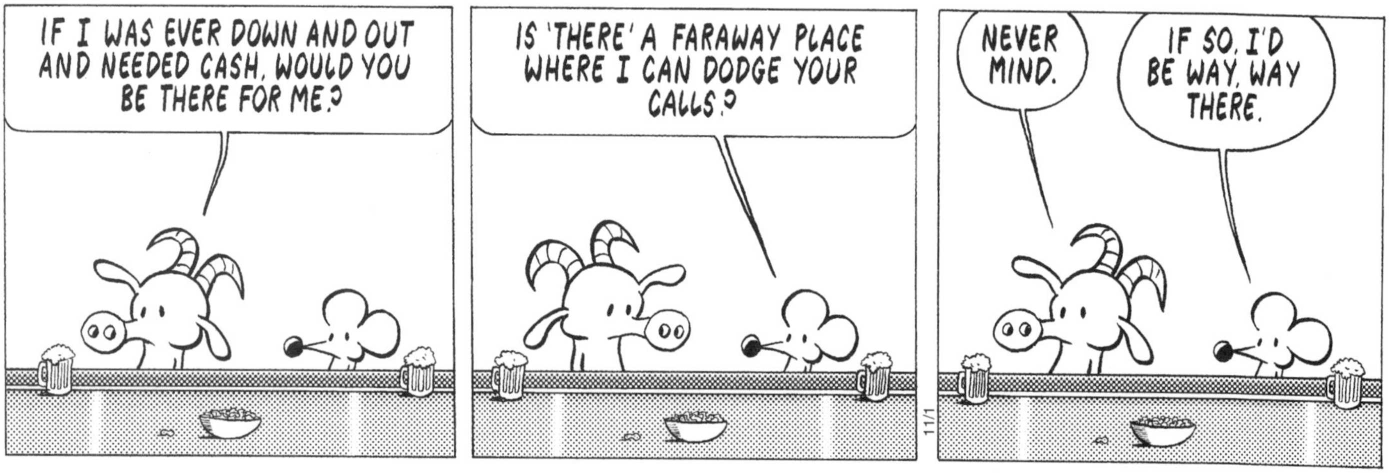
IF I WAS EVER DOWN AND OUT AND NEEDED CASH, WOULD YOU BE THERE FOR ME?
IS 'THERE' A FARAWAY PLACE WHERE I CAN DODGE YOUR CALLS?
NEVER MIND.
IF SO, I'D BE WAY, WAY THERE.
11/1

Thank goodness I have my wife, Staci. She's the one who makes all these calls for our family. On the downside, she makes me eat out of a dog bowl on the porch.

In that first panel, I wanted to have Marty mention that he had shot someone. But every time I mention shooting, people write letters to the newspaper. And some papers might not even run it.

I'm not sure what the chicken on the very top of the couch is staring at. But it seems inappropriate.

I found this strip funny. This reader did not:

I really do have a good sense of humor, but this strip is not humorous to me at all. Please consider dropping this topic.

You know what I bet? That she really doesn't have a good sense of humor.

All of these are actual streets in my hometown of Santa Rosa, California.

121

Unhappy being alone, Elly Elephant wanted a man who would listen.

So she dated and dated until she finally found him.

And when she found him, she knew immediately that he was the right man.

Because he listened.

For an hour.

And didn't judge. And didn't offer advice. And didn't brag.

11/9

A dream date. Marred only by the paramedics.

Who informed her that her great listener had died an hour ago.

Elly Elephant learned to be happy alone.

If you're wondering if I just cut and pasted that image of Elly in the first panel to use again in the last panel, the answer is most decidedly yes.

Aww. Sometimes you just want to hug Pig. Who is created by me. So really, you just want to hug me.

I didn't think I could get away with the phrase "take a whizz." But I did. So while Galileo made it safe to say that the earth revolves around the sun, I made it safe to say "take a whizz" on the comics page. Two pioneers.

Second panel: My view of life, neatly summed up in one comic strip panel.

If you or your loved ones are making a trip around America anytime soon, please feel free to use Panel 5 as a map. It is extraordinarily accurate.

This is one of the strangest series I've ever done in *Pearls*. That said, I really liked it.

Around this time, I grew very tired of drawing all these people. That's the problem with drawing a comic strip. Sometimes it involves drawing.

WHAT ARE YOU DOING, PIG?

SOMEONE HURT MY FEELINGS. AND WHENEVER THAT HAPPENS, I PLANT A FIG TREE. IT'S MY WAY OF TURNING A NEGATIVE INTO A POSITIVE.

HOPE YOU LIKE FIGS.

WHAT HAPPENED HERE, PIG?

I PLANTED A FIG TREE FOR EVERY TIME SOMEONE HAS HURT ME, BUT SOMEONE HAS GONE THROUGH AND EATEN ALL THE FIGS.

BUT THAT'S A TON OF FIG TREES, PIG. WHO COULD EAT THAT MANY FIGS?

EAT, MY PEOPLE.

Mysteriously, the faceless people have all grown mouths. I am nothing if not consistent.

WHATCHA DOING, RAT?

I'M HYPNOTIZING MYSELF. THE DOCTOR SAID IT MIGHT HELP ME GET RID OF ALL THESE FACELESS PEOPLE THAT FOLLOW ME.

OH. THEN I'LL BE QUIET.

GOOD. BECAUSE RIGHT NOW MY BRAIN IS VERY OPEN TO THE POWER OF SUGGESTION.

PILLSBURY CRESCENT ROLLS... MADE WITH THE FINEST PILLSBURY DOUGH.

THAT INCLUDES THE T.V.

SORRY.

Tee Hee

I have never heard from anyone at Pillsbury telling me that they enjoy my humor. Perhaps that's because the last time I showed the Pillsbury Doughboy, he was kicking Pig in the testicles.

That poor man really got socked. Get it? And that's why they pay me the big money.

LOOK, RAT... I GOT THIS UN-BELIEVABLE G.P.S... IT GIVES ME GUIDANCE AS TO WHAT STREETS TO TAKE, THE SHORTEST ROUTE, EVERYTHING.

BIG DEAL. ALL THOSE THINGS GIVE THAT KIND OF GUIDANCE.

AVOID THE RAT. HE BRINGS YOU DOWN.

IT DOES MORE.

My son messed with my GPS and made it so the voice is now that of a British man. So every time I make a wrong turn, I feel like Prince Charles is yelling at me.

HEY, GOAT, WANT TO SEE MY NEW G.P.S.? IT GUIDES ME EVERYWHERE.

NOT RIGHT NOW, PIG. TOO DEPRESSED. THIS GIRL I MET ONLINE JUST CANCELED OUR FIRST DATE.

LIFE OF LONELINESS AHEAD IN ONE MILE.

BAD G.P.S.

WHAT ARE YOU DOING, STEPH?

WRITING DOWN A LIST OF THINGS I WANT TO DO IN DUBLIN. I'M GOING THERE THIS MONTH.

OH, DUBLIN IS LOVELY! SAINT STEPHEN'S GREEN, TRINITY COLLEGE, THE JAMES JOYCE CENTER, ST. PATRICK'S CATHEDRAL...WHAT DO YOU HAVE ON YOUR BIG LIST SO FAR?

Drink Guinness.

TELL ME ABOUT THAT CHURCH THINGIE.

I traveled to Dublin a couple years ago. And one night, after a long day of drinking, I walked into a bar and asked if I could get a glass of water. The Irish bartender just stared at me and said, "You've got to be kidding." So I ordered a beer.

We really do go to my wife's relatives' house for Thanksgiving. And one year, my son and I brought this video game we were really good at called *NBA Jam*, which we carefully wrapped in cellophane as though it were brand new. We then challenged Staci's cousins to a game, acting like we were all learning the game for the first time. I think the score was 50 to 4 when they quit.

There's apparently some device you can now buy that you attach to the back of the airline seat in front of you, preventing it from reclining. But on a flight from Newark to Denver, it led to such a big fight between passengers that the plane had to be diverted to Chicago.

When bereavement fares were still offered (they're really not anymore), you had to show the airline proof of kinship and proof of death. So I guess that meant you had to take a photo of yourself standing in front of the coffin and waving.

And now, wherever you go today, and whatever you do, you will be hearing that song.

I don't listen to a lot of punk music, but sometimes, when I'm trying to write and want to get fired up, I listen to the Sex Pistols' version of "My Way."

While my personality *is* lacking, my toes are just fine.

This was inspired by a niece of mine who was invited to a friend's wedding in Hawaii. As far as I know, she did not write "deceased" on the envelope.

This, too, was inspired by one of my nieces, who was complaining about not being able to get a job without experience, and not being able to get experience without a job.

If you were wondering if vegans have a sense of humor about strips like this, wonder no more:

Dear Stephen,
Your Victor the Vegan character . . . must come from your deep well of guilt and shame that you feel due to
your complicity in the destruction of the environment and innocent lives because of your food choices.

The truth is that I feel neither guilt nor shame. But I do wish she'd spell my name correctly.

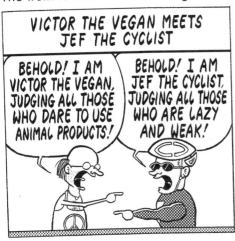

Another strip. Another complaint:

Dear Mr. Pastis,
Why are you so angry at vegans? I have at my fingertips hundreds of choices of food that do not harm
animals. Why are we the target of your anger?

Answer: Because I'm a cartoonist. And everyone is the target of my anger.

No Cossacks complained. So if you're keeping score at home about who has a good sense of humor, the score
is now: Cossacks: 1 Vegans: 0.

That bottle next to me is supposed to be suntan lotion. Though it could just as easily be mayonnaise.

This really did happen to my watch on a trip to Texas. Then one of the hands fell off entirely and the whole thing stopped working. I still wear the watch, though. Mostly because I like it when people ask me what time it is and I get to answer, "Sorry. My watch doesn't tell time."

RAT'S PRESIDENTIAL PLATFORM

If elected President of the United States, I, Rat, will buy 7,000,000,000 drones.

That is the number of people on earth.

Each drone will keep an eye on one person.

Monitoring everything that person does.

And listening in on every phone call.

And if that person does something displeasing, the drone will address the situation.

12/14

KABOOM

P.S. I will control all the drones.

I DON'T THINK I'LL VOTE FOR YOU.

YOUR DRONE WILL BE VERY AGGRESSIVE.

I'M EATING BREAKFAST, DRONE!

In the panel that contains the earth, those people are not quite to scale.

WHAT ARE YOU DOING, GOAT?

READING ANCIENT GREEK PHILOSOPHY. I DO IT WHEN LIFE GETS A BIT OVERWHELMING AND I NEED ANSWERS.

I HAVE A PHILOSOPHY I TURN TO IN TIMES LIKE THAT, TOO.

OH, YEAH? WHICH ONE?

EAT GALLON OF ICE CREAM.

IT'S INTELLECTUALLY SOUND.

HEY, VICTOR THE VEGAN. HOW GOES IT?

I CONDEMN THEE FOR PUTTING HONEY ON YOUR TOAST. HONEY IS AN ANIMAL PRODUCT AND YOU ARE SCUM.

SAID VICTOR WHILE SITTING ON A LEATHER DINER STOOL.

FORGIVE ME, GREAT COW IN THE SKY!

CAN HE SQUIRT SOME MILK IN MY COFFEE?

Once I knew the world was filled with humorless vegans, I felt compelled to do more strips.

I HAVE A LARGE BRAIN. AND IT'S BEEN CONCLUSIVELY PROVEN THAT THOSE WITH LARGER BRAINS ARE SMARTER THAN THOSE WITH SMALLER BRAINS.

THAT'S NOT TRUE.

YES, IT IS.

HOW DO YOU KNOW?

BECAUSE SOMETHING IS TRUE WHENEVER YOU SAY, 'IT'S BEEN CONCLUSIVELY PROVEN.'

THAT'S NOT HOW THAT WORKS.

HEY, IN AN AGE WHERE NO ONE READS, IT'S HOW THAT WORKS.

Speaking of brains, I actually did really well in school. But when I tell my kids that, they laugh.

I was one of the slowest runners on the cross country team. My only goal was to walk part of the course without my coach catching me. At that I succeeded.

Great movie. If you haven't seen it, you really should.

12/21

This strip was inspired by an actual call made by a cable customer to Comcast, where the Comcast representative made it extraordinarily hard for the customer to cancel his service. If you haven't heard it, Google it. It is unbelievable.

I'm not sure how many people got the Nancy Kerrigan–Tonya Harding reference. But you can Google that as well. I am nothing if not educational.

Aww. More touching Christmas strips. And by "touching," I mean getting whacked over the head with a baseball bat.

RAT'S WAR ON CHRISTMAS

WHAT ARE YOU DOING, PIG?

WATCHING SANTA'S REINDEER. THEY'RE DOING THEIR BUSINESS ALL OVER OUR FRONT LAWN.

AND I'M NOT EVEN GONNA USE THE POOPER SCOOPER!!!

SANTA CAN BE SO VINDICTIVE.

We have deer at our house. Somehow when they poop, they create little round balls, almost like tiny black marbles. I wish I could do that.

I KEEP TRYING TO CHANGE EVERYTHING IN MY LIFE. WHERE I TRAVEL. WHAT I SEE. WHERE I LIVE. BUT NONE OF IT MAKES ME ANY HAPPIER.

WHY IS THAT?

BECAUSE WHEREVER I GO, THERE I STILL AM.

I JUST BLEW MY OWN MIND.

My very first attempt at syndication was a six-panel strip just called *Rat*. One of those strips contained the line, "Wherever I go, there I still am." I liked it, so I borrowed from myself and used it almost 20 years later in *Pearls*.

RAT, THIS IS MY FRIEND, BILL...HE MAY HAVE KILLED A MAN, BUT IT'S OKAY BECAUSE THE COPS SAY HE'S A REALLY INTERESTING PERSON.

PERSON-OF-INTEREST.

I WAS CLOSE.

This is the main reason I almost never stay at other people's houses. The other reason is that they don't invite me.

LOOK AT THIS BIG AD FOR TRUCK MUDFLAPS. WHAT'S A MUDFLAP?

THESE RUBBER SQUARES THAT PROTECT OTHERS FROM THE HARMFUL DEBRIS THE TRUCK STIRS UP AS IT TRAVELS.

CAN WE PUT SOME ON MY MOTHER?

NO.

HER CHRISTMAS VISITS ARE VERY PAINFUL.

WHAT ARE YOU DOING, VICTOR THE VEGAN?

FORAGING THE FOREST FLOOR FOR NUTS AND BERRIES, LIVING AS NATURE INTENDED, INSTEAD OF HARMING OTHER CREATURES.

AND THE BEAR WASN'T A VEGAN.

Oh, no. Now I've gone and killed the poor vegan. I must have a deep well of guilt and shame.

WHAT HAPPENED TO YOU?

THIS HOMELESS-LOOKING GUY WAS ROAMING DOWN THE STREET WITH A SCYTHE, SO I HAD TO PUNCH HIM IN THE HEAD TO STOP HIM.

YOU BEAT UP FATHER TIME.

OH, WELL. IT WAS A BAD YEAR ANYWAYS.

Another holiday-related strip. And another violent episode. Clearly, I do not like the holidays.

In the early days of the strip, I was warned by at least one editor about telegraphing profanity too blatantly, such as here, where it's obvious that Rat is saying "bullsh#t." But this being 2014, I got away with it. It seems to me that while newspapers are still pretty conservative, they are less so than they were ten years ago.

When I meet readers at book signings, a lot of them tell me that they read their *Pearls* books when they're using the toilet. If that applies to you reading this right now, I hope things are going well.

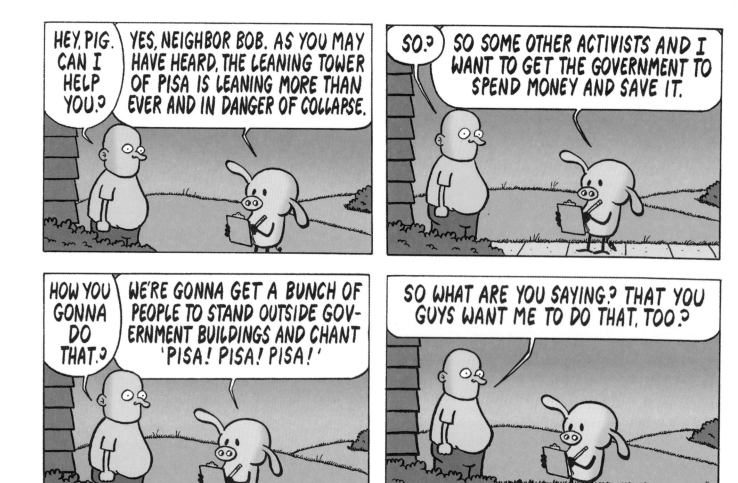

This was one of the more popular pun strips. I like it because the pun panel reads so naturally (i.e., it's not too much of a stretch), and it really does sound exactly like "Give Peace a Chance."

I'm not quite sure how Rat is carrying that laptop. It appears to be magically stuck to his right hand. I hope that did not detract from your enjoyment of the strip.

I worried a bit that at least one editor really would fill in the name of their local football team, which would have destroyed the joke. But if that happened somewhere, I didn't hear about it.

So one day I'm looking at police in the news. And they looked a lot more like soldiers in a war than everyday police officers. So I did a strip about it. And the response really took me by surprise:

With the recent liberal media's drubbing of our police and the murder of two NY officers, I didn't expect a cheap shot from you. Mistakenly, I had viewed you to be pretty broad minded & sensitive. I guess even educated writers never escape their elitist, stereotypical-anti-establishment, Berkeley mindset.

And here's another reader:

The January 9 strip was a cheap shot. You deftly "tossed under the bus" some of the folks who are willing to put their lives on the line to protect your right to disparage them.

And another:

As a former police officer . . . I found your comic of the 9th of January to be in very poor taste.

I think the reason for the response was that the issue of police brutality had been in the news a lot in the prior few weeks, and they figured that my strip was a comment on that. But my strip was drawn *six months prior to that*. It just sort of reinforced something I learned when the strip first started, which is that people are going to read into your strip what they want to read into your strip.

After this strip ran, I was contacted by Ken Burns's office and told that Ken liked this strip and wanted to buy the original. I sent it to him, and in exchange I got a cool signed book and a DVD of his series *The Roosevelts*.

I'VE CONCLUDED THAT TO BE ALIVE IS TO SUFFER.

AND THAT THE ELIMINATION OF THAT SUFFERING IS THE KEY TO ACHIEVING INNER PEACE.

THUS, BEER.

I'M NOT SURE IF I'M A PHILOSOPHER OR A DRUNK.

Around the time I wrote this one, I had been reading various books on Buddhism, and I think it sort of crept into the strip here. I am often influenced by the books I read. As a creative person, I think your output is only as good as your input.

DID YOU KNOW THE EARTH IS ONLY 5,000 YEARS OLD?

WHERE'D YOU HEAR THAT?

ON THE INTERNET.

YOU KNOW, PIG, NOT EVERYTHING YOU READ ON THE INTERNET IS TRUE.

THAT WAS MORE THAN HE COULD TAKE.

Pig's reaction in the third panel makes me laugh.

DID YOU SEE THAT NEW YORK'S TRYING TO PROSECUTE THIS GUY FOR ROBBERY, BUT IT CAN'T?

WHY NOT?

THE GUY'S AN AMBASSADOR FROM ANOTHER COUNTRY, SO HE HAS DIPLOMATIC IMMUNITY FOR ANY CRIME HE MIGHT COMMIT.

HE'S LIVING THE DREAM!

NO.

SOME THINGS YOU JUST DON'T TELL HIM.

Rat's line in the last panel is loosely based on the famous quote from the movie *The Princess Bride*: "You killed my father. Prepare to die."

I may have used this joke before. If so, it is only because I totally forgot and not because I have become creatively lazy. I would look through the archives to be sure, but that requires too much effort.

152

I'm not quite sure why that bush in the background is orange. Perhaps it's not a bush. Perhaps it's a pile of Cheetos.

WHERE WERE YOU LAST WEEK, STEPH?

I VISITED MONTREAL. BIKED THROUGH THE PLATEAU. WALKED THE STREETS OF OLD MONTREAL. CLIMBED MOUNT ROYAL.

SOUNDS LIKE TOO MUCH EXERCISE. DID YOU DO ANYTHING ELSE?

I ATE POUTINE, WHICH IS A BIG BOWL OF FRENCH FRIES SMOTHERED IN CHEESE CURDS AND GRAVY AND SOMETIMES PILED HIGH WITH SMOKED MEAT.

I AM MOVING TO MONTREAL!!

YOU HAD HIM AT CHEESE CURDS.

GRANT ME ASYLUM, YOU LOVELY POUTINE PEOPLE!!

I know a person in Montreal named Andy Nulman, who is a fan of *Pearls* and more importantly, very well-connected. So when I told him I was going there and wanted to see a Canadiens hockey game, he gave me the most ridiculously awesome tickets ever—front row, right next to the penalty box. All he asked was that I do a brief interview and draw something related to the team (which I think they were going to auction for charity). What I didn't expect was that they then asked me to draw it right before the game, while I was in my seat and pucks were banging off the glass in front of me. Long story short—I choked and drew one of the lamest drawings of my life, all while cameras filmed me. I felt really bad and wanted to make up for it, so when I got home, I created this strip, which promotes both Montreal and the team. And to my great surprise, it got a terrific response, including a reaction from the mayor of Montreal. If you Google "Mayor of Montreal" and "Pearls Before Swine," you can see him hanging the original strip on his office wall.

HOW DO YOU KNOW IF A PERSON YOU WANT TO MARRY IS THE RIGHT PERSON?

WELL, PIG, YOU DO YOUR BEST, BUT I'M AFRAID IT'S A BIT OF A COIN FLIP.

AND IF THE COIN LANDS ON ITS EDGE, YOU'VE FOUND THE RIGHT PERSON.

YOU'RE RATHER CYNICAL.

HEY, IT'S NOT IMPOSSIBLE.

I SHALL NEVER MARRY ANYONE!!

And this was the second of the two Montreal strips I created, for the same reason as above. If you look really closely at the bag, you'll see it says "St. Viateur Bagels." It's a famous bagel place in Montreal and they make the best bagels I've ever had in my life. And, like what happened with the prior strip, if you Google "St. Viateur Bagels" and "Pearls Before Swine," you'll see the owner hanging the original of this strip on the wall of his store. Man, I love Montreal.

This strip was surprisingly popular, proving once again that I never know which strips will work and which won't.

Apparently, this really is an issue with owning parrots. As a result, many of them outlive their owners.

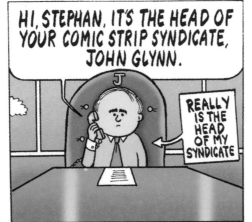

1/25

When I turn in a Sunday strip to the syndicate, it has two files: One is the black-and-white drawing, and one is the color file. In 15 years of drawing the strip, I've never had a problem with the color file. Until this strip. The syndicate said the file was corrupted and couldn't be read, causing me to have to recolor the entire strip. Am I suspicious that it just so happened to occur on a strip where I make fun of John Glynn, the head of the syndicate? You bet I am. I'm hoping that one day conspiracy theorists make a film about it.

There really are fruitarians. And that makes me sad.

I really did go to Australia. And I really did see kangaroos. And then I ate one. Victor the Vegan would not be pleased.

Every year I tell myself I need to buy an emergency preparedness kit. And then I never buy it. I think I'll just wait for an emergency.

If I go to a cafe and the only seat available is at a communal table, I leave and go to another cafe. Interaction with other humans is bad.

159

I really do wonder why we root for professional sports teams. College sports I can understand, particularly if you went to that college. But with pro teams, you really are rooting for one rich guy's company to beat another's.

I have never had a caramel macchiato. That's not particularly interesting, but I couldn't think of anything else to write here.

Someone really needs to start making these. We can't all be number one.

161

How exactly does Pig's tie work? It's not tied around his neck. And if it's a clip-on, it has nothing to clip on to. Maybe he just superglues it to his chest.

No Sikhs complained. Though perhaps no Sikhs read the strip. If you are a Sikh who reads the strip, please complain so I know you're out there.

Look at that beautiful sunrise I created. Or sunset. Whatever it is, it's beautiful.

GUARD DUCK FOUND OUT THAT THE CHEF HERE STILL SERVES FOIE GRAS, WHICH IS THAT FATTY DUCK LIVER THEY CREATE BY FORCE-FEEDING THE DUCK WITH A TUBE.

DOES THAT HURT?

WE'LL SEE.

IT LOOKS LIKE IT HURTS.

CHEW, FATTY, CHEW!

HEY, RAT... WHO CROSSED ALL THE TUESDAYS OFF OUR CALENDAR?

I DID. EVERYTHING BAD THAT'S EVER HAPPENED HAS HAPPENED ON A TUESDAY.

SO YOU JUST GOT RID OF THEM?

YES. SO NOW WE GO STRAIGHT FROM MONDAY TO WEDNESDAY.

OUR MONTH MAY BE A LITTLE QUICK.

NO IT WON'T. I ADDED FRIDAYS.

I really do have a fear of Tuesdays. It seems everything bad that happens to me happens on that day. And oddly, I was born on a Tuesday. So go figure.

WHY ARE YOU SO LATE?

THE POLICE BLOCKED OFF THE STREETS. THEY SAID THEY WERE CHASING SOME LAW-BREAKER. BUT I DON'T EVEN KNOW WHAT A LAWBREAKER IS.

HOW DUMB CAN YOU BE? THE WORD TELLS YOU EVERY-THING YOU NEED TO KNOW. A LAWBREAKER IS SOMEONE WHO *BREAKS* THE *LAW*.

SO MY WINDBREAKER BREAKS WIND?

PLEASE SIT SOMEWHERE ELSE.

I AM SO RETURNING THIS THING.

Why Pig sometimes wears clothes and sometimes doesn't is something I cannot explain.

HEY THERE, GOAT. DID YOU LIKE THE BIRTHDAY CAKE I SENT YOU?

I LOVED IT, PIG! THAT WAS VERY KIND OF YOU.

AND DID YOU SEE I GOT YOU THOSE CANDLES THAT YOU THINK YOU'VE BLOWN OUT, BUT THEN THEY RE-LIGHT?

THOSE WERE TRICK CANDLES?

IT'S THE THOUGHT THAT COUNTS.

After I wrote this, I learned that this really does happen. In one instance, people blew out the birthday candles and then discarded them. The candles then reignited in the trash can and burned down the house. The lesson here: Never celebrate birthdays.

HEY, NEIGHBOR BOB. HOW GOES IT?

GOOD. WHY ARE YOU DRESSED UP?

MATING SEASON BEGINS TODAY.

ZEBRAS HAVE A MATING SEASON?

YEAH. DON'T HUMANS?

IS 'ANYTIME I CAN GET IT' A SEASON?

SOUNDS MORE LIKE A PRAYER.

GENERALLY.

I was sort of surprised I got away with this one. Clearly, standards are slipping.

HEY JEN...MATING SEASON BEGINS TODAY AND I WAS WONDERING IF YOU'D LIKE TO GET A DRINK.

SURE. LET'S GO ON SEPTEMBER FIRST.

MATING SEASON ENDS THE LAST DAY OF AUGUST.

YEP.

MATING SEASON CAN BE CRUEL.

Ironically, independent bookstore sales have really begun to pick up. And the sale of vinyl records has taken off as well. So who knows, maybe everything is just cyclical.

166

That harp actually looks like a harp. I find that rather amazing.

Hey, the coffee does not cost $2.00. It costs $2.75. And I do not stay for three hours. I stay for two hours and 45 minutes.

THE CITY COUNCIL IS TRYING TO CHANGE THE WAY THE CITY IS GOVERNED, BUT THEY MOVE SO SLOWLY. OH, WELL... I GUESS ROME WASN'T BUILT IN A DAY.

OH, I'M SORRY, PIG... DO YOU KNOW WHAT THAT EXPRESSION MEANS?

ROME HAD LAZY CONTRACTORS?

NO.

THOSE PEOPLE NEVER FINISH WHEN THEY SAY THEY'LL FINISH!!

Whenever we hire a contractor to do something in our house, I take whatever his time estimate is and double it. That almost always turns out to be the actual completion time.

WHAT ARE YOU DOING, GOAT?

STARING AT THE WALRUSES ON THOSE ROCKS. THEY'RE JUST SO BEAUTIFUL AND MAJESTIC.

GET IN SHAPE, YOU FAT @#6# !

CYCLISTS AND WALRUSES DON'T MIX.

HEY FATTY... EVER HEARD OF A TREADMILL?

WHAT ARE YOU WATCHING, RAT?

THESE INSECURE PEOPLE WITH VARIOUS ADDICTIONS BEING REASSURED THAT THEY'RE OKAY AND THAT THEIR LIVES HAVE VALUE.

WHAT'S IT CALLED?

THE ACADEMY AWARDS.

AT LEAST THEY'RE PRETTY.

THEY CLEAN UP NICELY.

Ooh, snap. Take that, Hollywood.

2/22

I have two really nice cameras that I have not taken out of the closet in years. It's just so much easier to carry around my phone. Sorry, camera-selling guys.

I just finished watching a Netflix documentary on the motivational speaker Tony Robbins. It was both fascinating and terrifying. You really should see it.

I did not get paid for that last endorsement. But if anyone would like to pay me for an endorsement, I'll gladly sell out.

Buy Lawry's cinnamon! It's the best cinnamon out there! So go out and get some today!

After this strip ran, the Trailer Park Boys thanked me for the mention on Facebook. I absolutely love the show and have seen every episode. Bubbles and Ricky and Randy are some of the best characters ever created.

I was hoping to hear from U.C. Berkeley (I graduated from there), but I did not. I thought about stopping my donations to the school, but then I remembered I've never donated to the school.

I wrote this strip after seeing a TED Talk on whether we should still be making kids memorize facts in the age of the smartphone. The point of the talk was that we should be teaching kids *how* to think instead. And if you're a kid who is supposed to be studying right now for a history final, you probably just screamed, "Hallelujah!"

After fading out the "lemming on a cliff" gag, I thought it might be a good idea to bring just one of them back as a regular character. So I did. But it only lasted for a few strips.

I think the Romanian dog just wanted to be fed.

I like this strip, but the next one is really lame. Please don't look at it.

You looked at it. Even though I asked you not to. You've really destroyed the trust in our relationship.

Apologies to anyone out there who really does have a dolphin tattoo.

HEY, PIG, WHERE WERE YOU?

AT THAT NEW JAMES BOND-THEMED RESTAURANT. THE SERVERS ARE ALL BOND VILLAINS AND EACH CONTROLS A DIFFERENT FACTION OF THE RESTAURANT.

SOUNDS FUN.

YEAH. AND EACH SERVER WILL ONLY SIT YOU IN THEIR AREA IF YOU KNOW A LOT ABOUT THE MOVIE THEY WERE IN.

REALLY?

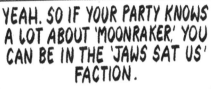
YEAH. SO IF YOUR PARTY KNOWS A LOT ABOUT 'MOONRAKER,' YOU CAN BE IN THE 'JAWS SAT US' FACTION.

I SEE.

LIKE I CAN GET INTO 'GOLDFINGER SAT US' FACTION BECAUSE I KNOW A LOT ABOUT 'GOLDFINGER.'

THAT'S GREAT. IS DR. NO THERE?

YEAH, BUT I DON'T KNOW A LOT ABOUT THE 'DR. NO' FILM.

SO?

3/8

SO I CAN'T GET 'NO SAT US' FACTION.

WOULD YOU RATHER BE SHAKEN OR STIRRED?

Oh, man, I had to go a long way to make this pun work. Probably too long. The good news is that Pig looks quite handsome in a tuxedo.

One more strip for my friends in Montreal.

Have you ever seen those people on Facebook who post hundreds and hundreds of photos of their own face? They frighten me.

I like it best when the pun sounds exactly like the real sentence, like here ("I herd it through the grapevine"). I can only do that when the pun is really simple, like it is in this strip.

My best advice to everyone out there: When in doubt, don't click "send."

177

I do not have shallow friends. That is because I do not have any friends at all. Well, except for my friend Emilio. But he's not that smart, so I'm not sure if I can count him.

I just called my friend Emilio and told him about that last comment. He said if I don't change it, he is going to punch me as hard as he can the next time he sees me. I think the solution here is to never show him the book.

I am very good at avoiding people. Which is good, because for the next few years, I may have to avoid Emilio.

I do occasionally bite off the end of string cheese. It's a big time-saver.

I just weighed myself and discovered that I am 202 pounds, the most I have ever weighed. The only thing I can figure out is that perhaps the iPhone in my pocket weighs 30 pounds.

For those of you who are too young to remember this, the Time Lady was this number you called if you wanted to know what time it was. She would say, "At the tone the time will be . . . 8:35 and twenty seconds." And then on and on, every ten seconds. It was sort of mesmerizing.

I have never gone skydiving. But in 1989, I fell off the Leaning Tower of Pisa. It happened as I was climbing back down the stairs that lead to the ground. I tripped on the second-to-last step and fell. The fall was about a foot and a half down. But still, I fell off the Leaning Tower of Pisa.

On my recent trip to Australia, I got to see a lot of koalas. For those of you who have never seen a koala in person and are ready for some nonstop koala action, let me prepare you in advance: They do nothing but sleep.

This was inspired by the shipping company that often delivers packages to our house. They frequently leave the packages at the foot of our driveway where they can be stolen, driven over, rained upon, etc. This is why I told Bill Watterson not to ship me the finished strips we drew together. I was petrified they would be ruined.

In the days before Google Maps and GPS, people would often pull over and ask other people for directions. I would always try to help, but afterwards I'd walk away and think, "Oh, crap. I told them the wrong thing." God only knows the number of hours I cost people.

I absolutely hate it when you have a meaningful goodbye filled with hugs and tears, and then you have to drive back ten minutes later and say, "Hey, sorry, did I leave my sunglasses in your kitchen?"

If asparagus tasted like cheese puffs, I'd eat a lot of asparagus. But that's the problem. It tastes too much like asparagus.

Whenever I use a first and last name, I try to make the last name as unusual as possible, thereby diminishing the odds that there really is a person with that last name out there. Because if there is, that person will think you wrote the strip about them and want to know why. Or they will ask for the original. Or both. So if there really is a Melvin Melvinowitz out there, no, this was not about you.

185

I didn't intend for this to happen, but I see now that this strip was a good follow-up to the prior day's strip. Rat is trying to do things for others. Sort of.

And this is a good follow-up also! That's very odd. See, when I determine what strips will run on what day, I am generally looking at around 180 different strips spread out on the floor of my studio. Then I just grab strips randomly (unless they're part of a series or I need one for a specific holiday). And by sheer coincidence, these last two strips follow the April 1 strip perfectly. Very strange.

4/5

I've been playing a lot of Pokémon Go lately and boy does it eat up the battery. On the bright side, I catch a lot of those little monsters, thereby making the world safe for the rest of you.

When I was in elementary school, rainy days meant that we had to stay indoors and do one of two things: dance the hokey pokey in the lunchroom or watch *The Red Balloon*. If you've never watched *The Red Balloon*, let me tell you right now, it is one of the most depressing things you'll ever see. This little kid has a red balloon that he loves more than anything. Then some kid pops it. I think my elementary school was subtly teaching me that everything in life ends in destruction and sadness.

This is the kind of strip that would typically generate complaints. But in recent years, I've reduced the number of complaints I get by no longer printing my e-mail address between the panels of the strip. Another way to reduce complaints would be to be less offensive. But that seemed too hard.

The only reason I used this word was because I Googled "hardest words to pronounce" and "otolaryngology" was on the list. Fortunately, it's not one I use in everyday conversation.

Someone really should do a book on cartoon physics. It has its own set of rules.

189

I really do hug a lot more people when I'm drunk. It's like I become a giant Care Bear and the world is filled with nothing but other Care Bears.

This is the only time I have put my own son Thomas in the strip. Thomas is a shade under six foot six, and once a day someone asks him this series of questions.

Rat looks psychotic whenever he smiles.

For this joke to work, you have to know that that's a stork in the last panel. So I'm telling you now: That's a stork. It is not a flamingo or a swan.

I used to do this whenever I took my kids to the park. But it was okay, because every half hour or so I would text them and say, "Your father still loves you."

192

Based on past experience, I'm guessing that very few of these people use deodorant.
So the room probably smells as well.

THESE TWO RICH DOCTORS BUILT A COUPLE OF PIERS TO BRING MORE TOURISTS TO THE BEACH, BUT FOR REASONS THEY CAN'T EXPLAIN, IT'S ACTUALLY DRIVING TOURISTS AWAY.

HEY, GUYS, WHATCHA TALKING ABOUT?

A PAIR OF DOCS' PAIR OF DOCKS PARADOX.

MY MONDAY IS RUINED.

Oddly, if you look very closely at the second panel, you will see that Rat is reading a Pittsburgh newspaper. And I'm not sure there are many beaches in Pittsburgh.

WHAT ARE YOU DOING, LARRY?

Me hunting prey.

YOU'RE SITTING IN A LAWN CHAIR DRINKING BEER.

Me in planning phase.

No one respekk planning phase.

This is sort of from my own life. Because as a cartoonist, you truly do need to spend a lot of time relaxing and goofing around if you are going to try and write something funny. But to everyone else, it just looks like you are being lazy. Or maybe I am just being lazy. It's hard to tell.

HEY, PIG... I'M TAKING A POLL. DO YOU BELIEVE IN CREATIONISM OR EVOLUTION?

NEITHER.

WHY NEITHER?

BECAUSE IN THE TIME I'VE BEEN ALIVE, I'VE BECOME CERTAIN OF ONLY ONE THING.

WHAT'S THAT?

THAT I LIKE DONUTS.

ONE VOTE FOR DONUTS.

WHO DOESN'T VOTE FOR DONUTS?

194

Given that Rat doesn't wear pants, this is a very hard strip to figure out. Someone should write a letter to the cartoonist.

If you've ever gone to a protest rally, you'll find that many people who attend are smelly and strange. Someone should protest that.

After this strip ran, I posted it on Twitter and wrote, "Apologies to @espnSteveLevy, whose name just came in handy." Levy himself retweeted it and answered, "Happy to help."

196

Panel 1: HI, LIFEGUARD SUPERVISOR LENNY...HOW GOES YOUR JOB MANAGING LIFEGUARDS? / NOT GOOD. I HAVE JUST UNDER 100 PROBLEMATIC SWIMMING SITES TO MONITOR AND NOT ENOUGH LIFEGUARDS. I HAVE RIVERS, LAKES, POOLS, YOU NAME IT.

Panel 2: BEACHES? / NO. I GOT 99 PROBLEMS, BUT A BEACH AIN'T ONE.

Panel 3: I'M WATCHING YOU, PASTIS. / I KNOW.

The fact that I can get away with this shows how much newspapers have changed in recent years. There is no way they would have run this back when I started in 2002. Just no way.

Panel 1: WHAT ARE YOU DOING, RAT? / I GOT A JOB AS A POLL-TAKER.

Panel 2: DO YOU DO IT FAIRLY? / SURE. I JUST ASK THE QUESTION AND WRITE DOWN THE ANSWER. WATCH.

Panel 3: SIR, ARE YOU IN FAVOR OF THE CURRENT MAYOR OR DO YOU AGREE WITH ALL THE SMART PEOPLE WHO SAY HE'S A BIGTIME POOPHEAD?

Panel 4: THIS MAYOR'S IN TROUBLE.

Even "poophead" would have caused problems back then. No more.

Panel 1: I DON'T THINK YOU SHOULD BE A POLL-TAKER, RAT. I THINK YOU ASK QUESTIONS IN A BIASED WAY. / FINE. I'LL ASK MY QUESTION IN A TOTALLY NEUTRAL WAY.

Panel 2: DO YOU THREE APPROVE OF THE DIRECTION OF THE ECONOMY?

Panel 3: THEY DO NOT.

These really are my favorite three albums. With Van Morrison's *Astral Weeks* being a close fourth.

You cannot go wrong with a life of beer and tacos.

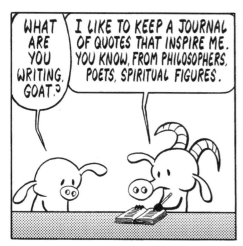

Angry Bob was angry.

So he went to see a life coach.

"You worry too much," said the life coach, "And you lead a sedentary life. You need to travel, seek adventure, seize the day."

So Angry Bob booked a trip to New Zealand.

There he hiked volcanos, surfed waves, and decided to overcome his fear of bungee jumping.

"Fear is stupid," he shouted from atop a high bridge as the bungee instructor attached the bungee cord to his leg.

"From now on, I'm going to live a new life! One where I seize the day!" Bob shouted as he jumped from the bridge...

5/3

...before the instructor could finish securing Bob's cord.

Bob's new life lasted four seconds.

NEVER SEIZE THE DAY.

I WILL SIT ON MY COUCH FOR LIFE!

This was inspired by my trip to New Zealand, which I visited while on a *Timmy Failure* book tour. It's one of the most beautiful countries I have ever seen.

199

In trying to make Rat sound like a Paleolithic man, I inadvertently made him talk like one of the crocs.

I chose Colorado here because it's one of only a few states to legalize marijuana (at least as of the time I'm writing this in 2016). While I was there, I may have purchased edibles. And afterwards, I may have spoken to a large group of people at the *Denver Post*. I don't recommend that course of conduct.

There really are new hairs growing out of each ear. They are unwelcome.

I think I could eat nachos every day for the rest of my life. With an occasional break for pizza. No wonder I weigh 202 pounds.

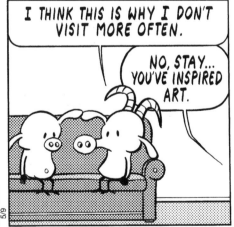

If you have a choice, always go to other peoples' houses instead of having them come to yours. Because if you go to their house, you can always leave when you get bored. But if they visit you and you get bored, you can't just lift them up and put them outside.

I really do have this superstition. Especially when watching sports. If someone in the room says something good is about to happen to my team (thereby jinxing them), everybody in the room has to knock. And not just any knock. But three sets of three knocks each (a total of nine knocks). And the knocks have to occur before the next play begins. Both of my kids now do it religiously, proving that I have seriously scarred them for life.

When someone talks on their phone in a restaurant or cafe, I just stare at them. Not in a threatening way, but in a friendly way, as if to say, "Thanks for including me in the conversation." I think they find it unsettling.

I have a springer spaniel named Edie. She is the sweetest dog ever, but I'm fairly certain she would march right over my dead body for a strip of bacon.

Well, the truth is that they send e-mails, not letters. But it's harder to draw a stack of e-mails.

bababadalgharaghtakammin-
arronnkonnbronntonnerronn-
tuonnthunntrovarrhouna-
wnskawntoohoohoordenen-
thurnuk!

WHOA. WHAT IS ALL THAT? IS YOUR KEYBOARD BROKEN?

THAT'S A QUOTE FROM THE JAMES JOYCE CLASSIC, 'FINNEGANS WAKE.'

OH. IT'S A FINE LINE BETWEEN CLASSIC LITERATURE AND A BROKEN KEYBOARD.

Believe it or not, that really is a quote from *Finnegans Wake*, proving once again that James Joyce's only goal in life was to frustrate the living crap out of all of us.

CAN I HELP YOU, MR. DEATH?

YEAH, PIG, YOUR KUMQUAT TREE IS DROPPING KUMQUATS ON MY LAWN. YOU NEED TO GO OVER THERE AND PICK THEM UP.

I'M SORRY, BUT I'M NOT GOING TO DO THAT.

I LOVE DEFYING DEATH.

I READ YOUR HUMOROUS BLOG ENTRY YESTERDAY. IT REALLY HAD ME R.O.T.F.

ROLLING ON THE FLOOR?

RUNNING OUTSIDE TO FLEE.

MY, IT GOT DARK.

5/17

I wrote this after watching a number of protests on the news where the first thing the protestors did was destroy local businesses, a counterproductive move if ever there was one.

Sadly, this is the most productive I can be.

The government really did put out a guide to roasting marshmallows. Makes me sad every time I pay taxes.

This strip has a very big error. See if you can find it yourself (answer in the next comment).

Answer to last question: In the last panel of the strip, the line of my shirt crosses right over Pig's ear. So either my body is magically transparent, or Pig's ear is.

5/24

I thought this strip was really funny. I loved the notion of a couple's fight being relayed via messages in a bottle. But it did not get a big reaction, proving once again that you just can't predict which strips will resonate and which won't.

Some people didn't get that the joke here was "salmonella outbreak." And when I say "some people," I mean one guy in particular who wrote to me. Maybe he just wasn't smart and all of the rest of you understood it.

There are advantages to living on the porch. For one thing, I never have to vacuum.

Rarely has a cartoonist depicted himself in such a lowly fashion. I'd complain, but I have no one to complain to.

I really do panic whenever I try these finger traps. And when you panic, you absolutely cannot get it off. There is something very sad about a child's toy causing a 48-year-old man to cry.

To all banks, insurance companies, computer makers, cable providers, and other big giganto corporations.

Thank you for your beautiful commercials filled with beautiful people telling me beautiful things about your beautiful company.

I can see from all these ads that you really want me to like you...
And I **WANT** to like you.

So here's a suggestion.

Sometimes I have to call you. And when I do, instead of spending all those billions on ads...

5/31

HAVE A LIVE, NON-ROBOTIC HUMAN IN THIS COUNTRY PROMPTLY PICK UP THE ⊚☆#⊚☆⊚# PHONE!!!!!

I THINK I BLEW OUT MY NERVOUS SYSTEM.

TOO BAD. THE HOLD TIME FOR OUR HEALTH INSURER IS TWELVE HOURS.

The truth is that I almost never have to make any of these calls, because my wife Staci takes care of all of them. She's very helpful that way. You can see now why she makes me live in a basket.

The crocs don't appear quite as much as they used to. Some people complain that they want to see them more. Some people want to see them less. And some people say they appear exactly the right amount of time and that I am a genius.

In regard to the comment under that last strip, the whole last sentence is a lie. I just said it to make myself feel good.

I got very good at Fruit Ninja. Then my son Thomas set a high score that was impossible to beat, so I gave up. The whole thing was very painful and I'd rather not talk about it.

212

He was even born with a backwards cap on his head. It's strange how genetics works.

The interesting point here is that you never see the little kid again. I have no idea what happened to him. I think that makes me a very poor parent.

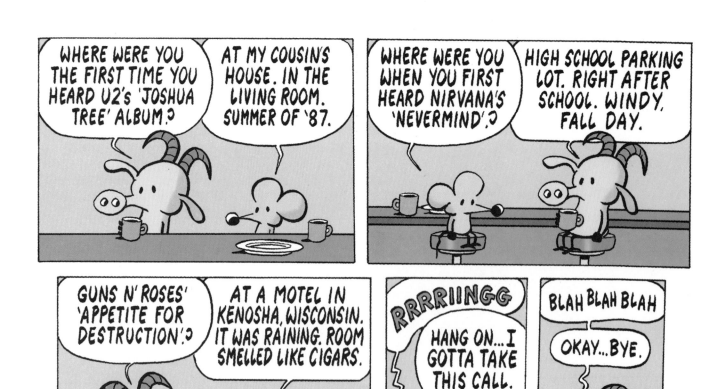

I really did stay in a smelly hotel room in Kenosha, Wisconsin. That was bad, but not as bad as when the construction on the floor above me woke me up at 8 a.m. Other than that, it was a lovely stay.

THE BIGGEST CITY IN NIGERIA IS TRYING TO IMPROVE THEIR ECONOMY BY PRODUCING FROZEN WAFFLES. THEIR LOGO IS JUST THE CITY'S NAME. AND TO PROMOTE THEM, THEY'RE PUTTING CHILDREN'S BUILDING BLOCKS IN EACH ONE.

LET'S GO.

LET'S GO WHAT?

LET'S GO GET LAGOS LOGO EGGO LEGOS.

LET'S NOT.

For the record, I do not have shirts that say "PASTIS" on them. Though I should.

WHATCHA DOING, RAT?

I TURNED THIS FLOWER POT INTO A SEAT. IT'S PRETTY COMFORTABLE.

LOOK...YOU CAN STAND ON IT, TOO.

NO YOU CAN'T. IT'LL BREAK. IT'S FOR SITTING ONLY.

REALLY?

YES! SIT OR GET OFF THE POT!

AREN'T YOU TWO CLEVER?

STAY OFF THE POT, CENSOR.

COMIC STRIP CENSOR

The expression here is "sh#t or get off the pot." And the reason that little "#" is in the middle of the word is because my editors won't let me say the word "sh#t." Look at that, they did it again.

HEY, BARTENDER... IS THIS PLACE NEW?

YES...IT'S A HIGH-END WHISKEY BAR. I RECOMMEND A SCOTCH BLEND DISTILLED AT LEAST THRICE AND AGED SIX YEARS IN OAK BARRELS... SERVED NEAT, OF COURSE, IN A TULIP-SHAPED GLASS TO PRESERVE THE AROMA.

ME WANT BEER.

I LIKE TO KEEP THE SNOBS IN THEIR PLACE.

Somebody recently took me to one of these high-end whiskey bars and I really did order a beer. I was not invited back.

215

The Cullinan Diamond truly is the world's largest diamond, and the Madagascar pochard really is the world's rarest bird, proving that this book can be educational. Though if this book is your idea of an education, you are in deep trouble.

Pearls Before Unclean Animals

In deference to those who say cartoonists should refrain from depicting anything that could cause offense to others, today we delete all of the Pearls characters who have ever caused offense to others.

It's interesting that the characters are well-defined enough that you can sort of tell who would be saying what. From left to right, I see the last panel as being Rat, me, and Pig.

6/14

The stripe on the man's sweater is my little tribute to Charles Schulz, the creator of *Peanuts*. It's the zig-zag stripe from Charlie Brown's shirt.

GUARD DUCK! YOU'VE BEEN GONE FOREVER! WHERE HAVE YOU BEEN?

I'VE RETIRED FROM THE MILITARY AND MOVED TO THE WOODS. NOW I'M WRITING A SCHOLARLY TREATISE ON MY TIME IN THE SERVICE.

SOUNDS IMPORTANT. CAN I SEE WHAT YOU HAVE SO FAR?

OF COURSE.

I blew $#!# up.

THE REST WILL BE FILLER.

The original idea for this was to have Guard Duck move to the woods and be there permanently as sort of a comic strip version of the Unabomber. But I got bored after just three strips and stopped.

SO WHY DID YOU DECIDE TO LIVE IN THE WOODS, L'IL GUARD DUCK?

BECAUSE I'M TIRED OF LIVING IN A WORLD WHERE WE TWEET OUR EVERY THOUGHT. SO I'M GOING OFF THE GRID. NO MORE FACEBOOK, TEXTING, E-MAIL, SMARTPHONES.

BUT WHAT IF IT'S AN EMERGENCY AND I REALLY NEED TO REACH YOU?

THAT'S WHERE THE PONY EXPRESS COMES IN.

AND I DON'T DO SMILEY-FACE EMOTICONS.

That's a horse in the last panel. For those of you wondering.

WHAT ARE YOU DOING, RAT?

PLAYING WITH TOY CARS. RIGHT NOW, THIS SPORTS CAR WITH THE GOLF CLUBS IN THE BACK IS CONTEMPLATING CRASHING INTO THIS GASOLINE TRUCK, THEREBY TRIGGERING A MAMMOTH EXPLOSION.

WHY WOULD THE GUY IN THE SPORTS CAR DO THAT?

HE'S FRUSTRATED BY HIS PUTTING GAME.

GOLFERS ARE A TIGHTLY WOUND BUNCH.

Whenever the characters get a bit philosophical, such as here, I put them at the shore staring out at the waves. Seems like a good place to meditate.

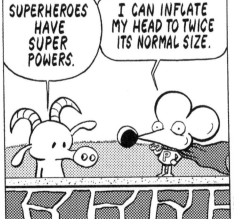

Pompous Boy was also going to be a regular character. But he appeared in just one strip and never appeared again. Which is not very regular.

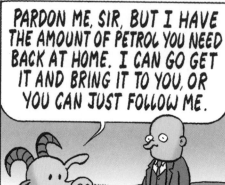

6/21

If you're ever in Britain and wear a little fanny pack around your waist, try not to call it a fanny pack. Fanny has a much different meaning in Britain.

That laundry basket looks so much like a laundry basket that I don't even feel the need to tell you it's a laundry basket.

True confession time: I really do watch *The Challenge* religiously. I think I've seen every single episode from every single season. Please. Don't judge.

If I remember right, this came from real life. I was driving down the freeway and there was a big "SELF STORAGE" sign and the light in the first "S" was burnt out.

Oh, I hate when people do this. Though unlike Rat, I have never kicked any of them in the knee.

Panel 1: PIG, I'D LIKE YOU TO MEET MY FRIEND, PROFESSOR BOB. HE HAS TENURE, SO HE HAS A LOT OF ACADEMIC FREEDOM. / WHICH MEANS WHAT?

Panel 2: THAT IT'S 'NO PANTS MONDAY.' / CENSORED

Panel 3: I FEAR TUESDAY.

For reasons that will never be clear to me, a lot of academic folk are truly offended by Professor Bob and these jokes about tenure. But it makes me laugh, so I do it anyway.

Panel 1: HEY, RAT, I'D LIKE TO GIVE YOU THIS INVITATION TO MY WEDDING. IT'S GOING TO BE A VERY ROMANTIC, FORMAL AFFAIR. / THANKS, NEIGHBOR BOB.

Panel 2: SO AS I UNDERSTAND IT, THIS REQUIRES ME TO RENT A TUX AND SPEND AT LEAST $150 FOR A GIFT, ALL FOR A LUKEWARM PIECE OF CHICKEN AND A SATURDAY WITH YOUR RELATIVES.

Panel 3: SO LET'S PRETEND THIS DIDN'T HAPPEN.

Panel 4: HE'S NOT SUPER ROMANTIC.

Neighbor Bob is no relation to Professor Bob. Despite the fact that they look almost exactly alike. I need to stop naming people Bob and drawing them identically.

Panel 1: SAVE ME, PIG...I'M A CHICKEN BREAST, AND IF THE FAST FOOD CHAINS GET AHOLD OF ME, THEY'LL CHOP ME INTO LITTLE NUGGETS. / AND YOU DON'T LIKE THAT?

Panel 2: NO...I DON'T EVEN KNOW WHAT A NUGGET IS. / THEN I'LL TRY TO GET THE FAST FOOD CHAINS TO STOP. DO YOU WANT ME TO KEEP YOU INFORMED OF MY EFFORTS?

Panel 3: YES, I'D APPRECIATE YOUR KEEPING ME ABREAST OF KEEPING ME A BREAST.

Panel 4: THIS STRIP SHOULD DIE A SLOW, PAINFUL DEATH.

224

This really happened in California. The polls showed that people were overwhelmingly in favor of this labeling, and then they voted against it. Maybe there should be an IQ test for voting.

There's a cartooning award (I won't say which one) where they encourage you to stuff the ballot in your own favor by getting your own fans to vote over and over for you. I'm not sure what that proves, other than you can cheat well.

Shout-out to Lagunitas Brewery in Petaluma, California. Great beer. And near where I live. And if that doesn't get me free beer, I don't know what will.

HEY, DAD...MOM WANTS TO KNOW IF YOU'RE GONNA HUNT ZEBRAS TODAY.

No. Nature say timing not right.

WHAT DOES THAT MEAN?

Me so drunk me can't walk.

I'LL TELL HER THAT NATURE THING.

Hey, who move chair?

Larry is me after Lagunitas gives me all that free beer.

HI, GOAT. IT'S ME, PIG. I'M AT YOUR HOUSE. SOME GUY NAMED 'YVES' IS HERE TO DESTROY YOUR GARAGE.

OH, YEAH. HE'S FROM 'DESTRUCTION INC.' THEY'RE GONNA DEMOLISH MY GARAGE SO I CAN BUILD A NEW ONE.

GEE, I THOUGHT HE WAS DOING SOMETHING BAD, SO RAT AND I HAVE BEEN STANDING ON TOP OF HIM TO PREVENT IT.

YOU'VE GOTTA BE KIDDING ME. YOU AND RAT AREN'T REALLY STANDING ON AN EMPLOYEE OF DESTRUCTION, INC., ARE YOU?

YOU DON'T BELIEVE WE'RE ON THE YVES OF DESTRUCTION?

I'D PREFER DESTRUCTION.

The pun in the third panel is based on a famous song from the 1960s. I'd look it up, but I'm on a plane as I write this and the Wi-Fi is bad and the flight attendant is mean.

THIS MAN'S LEAVING HIS WIFE FOR ACTING TOO MUCH LIKE AN ADULT.

THAT'S NOT THE MEANING OF ADULTERY.

I'm still on a plane. And the guy in front of me just reclined his seat all the way back. I seriously want to punch him in the head. But he's about six years old, so it would look bad.

I really do love Bill Bryson's books. If you've never read one, you should. He's hilarious and brilliant.

WHERE'S YOUR PHONE TODAY, GOAT?

I LEFT IT AT HOME. I'M TRYING NOT TO BE SO GLUED TO IT ANYMORE.

HOW COME?

I REALIZED THAT WHEN I HAVE IT ON ME, I'M NOT FULLY PRESENT FOR THE PEOPLE AROUND ME.

I DON'T HEAR THEIR CONVERSATION. I DON'T PAY ATTENTION TO THEIR CONCERNS.

SO I ACT LIKE I'M ENGAGED, BUT I'M NOT. I'M TOO FOCUSED ON ME.

MY APPS. MY PHOTOS. MY MUSIC. MY CONCERNS. EVERYTHING IS ME, ME, ME, ME, ME.

7/12

YOU JUST DESCRIBED HEAVEN.

I'M TELLING THIS TO THE WRONG GUY.

I WILL ENTOMB MYSELF BEHIND A WALL OF SMARTPHONES!

This has nothing to do with the strip. I just want to say that the little kid in front of me on the airplane is now using his seat as a trampoline. Good lord, now he's looking at me.

For what it's worth, I no longer have a goatee. And I'm not as fat as my character. And I don't wear a backwards baseball cap. And I don't have a big nose. Other than that, he looks exactly like me.

I really am an organ donor. Well, not yet. I think they wait until I die.

In the spring of 2015, I took a trip down Highway 61 through the blues country of Mississippi. It was one of the best trips of my life. I drank moonshine and sat on the back porch of an old sharecropper's cabin and listened to a local couple play the blues. It was awesome.

Okay, the little kid on the plane is staring at me again. And it really smells. So I think he farted. Though, in fairness, it might have been me.

While writing the strip one day, I sort of mindlessly drew Larry as a clown. I liked the way it looked, so I wrote a strip around it.

This really is scientifically true. If someone puts french fries in front of you, nature mandates that you eat every single one of them. The same goes for chips, bread, onion rings, cheese sticks, and donuts. It does not hold true for asparagus.

This was a very popular strip among bookstores. So if you have a local bookstore, try to shop there sometimes. Because if you don't, they will go away, and that would be bad.

233

This is me. I cannot fix a single thing. Though I don't always cry.

After this ran, Marc Maron tweeted about it. Which I thought was very cool, given how much I love his podcast.

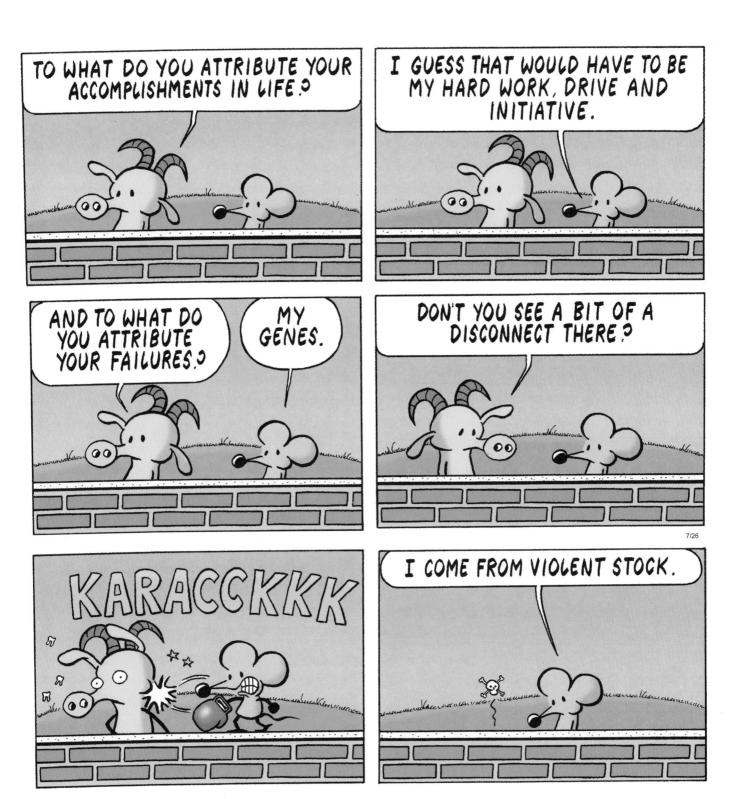

Goat's mouth is closed so I'm not quite sure how his teeth flew out of it. Give yourself five
Pearls points if you noticed that profound error.

Speaking of little turds, the kid in front of me on the plane is now crying. Would it be fair/ethical to put him in the overhead bin?

Okay, the word that kid is saying in the last panel is supposed to be "balls." But they wouldn't let me say that in newspapers. So I'm saying it now. And it feels very liberating.

HEY, TENURED PROFESSOR BOB, IS THERE ANY WAY FOR YOUR UNIVERSITY TO FIRE YOU? LIKE WHAT IF YOU TOOK A BOW AND ARROW AND SHOT A COLLEAGUE IN THE BACK?

HOW MANY TIMES?

I SEE.

LESS THAN THREE IS A REAL GRAY AREA.

I THOUGHT YOU WENT TO THE BASEBALL GAME.

I DID, BUT I GOT KICKED OUT FOR BRINGING ONE OF THOSE BALLS FOR THE CROWD TO KNOCK AROUND.

YOU MEAN A BEACH BALL? PEOPLE LOVE BEACH BALLS.

SIX PEOPLE WERE HOSPITALIZED.

I saw a great clip once on *SportsCenter* where a fan was trying to watch a game while people around him were knocking around a beach ball. So when it landed in his lap, he popped it.

WHAT'S YOUR BIGGEST FEAR?

TO DIE IN OBSCURITY, LIKE MY FATHER.

THAT DIDN'T HAPPEN TO MY FATHER.

HE DIDN'T DIE IN OBSCURITY?

NO, HE DIED IN CLEVELAND.

I LOVE THESE DEEP CONVERSATIONS.

I'm not sure but I think I may have recently done a strip involving Pig's father. Which would mean he is somehow alive again. I really need to keep track of these things.

I really like this strip.

It amaaaaaaaazes me that I got away with this. Truly. This is probably the furthest I've ever stretched the profanity limits.

When I was a kid, I buried a time capsule in our front yard. It was a bunch of *Time* magazine clippings in an envelope. I have a feeling that a paper envelope was not the most durable material with which to build a time capsule.

Technically, the expression is "in arrears," but that didn't work, so I changed the English language to suit my needs.

A 90-year-old woman in a coma might not be a bad date. For one thing, you'd never argue.

8/9

I do this all the time, particularly with lights. For example, when I leave my studio at the end of the day, I go back at least twice and check to make sure I turned the light off. And just last week, I found it on. So now I will check at least three times.

THIS POLITICIAN ONLY HAS A YEAR LEFT IN OFFICE AND HE CAN'T GET A SINGLE THING DONE. HE'S A REAL LAME DUCK.

THAT WAS CULTURALLY INSENSITIVE.

That really is a strange expression. Why pick on ducks? Why not lame cows?

GIMME.

NO.

HEY, NEIGHBOR NANCY, DO YOU MAKE YOUR KIDS SHARE THEIR WATER BOTTLES?

NOT IF IT'S AN OVERCAST DAY LIKE TODAY.

SO IF IT'S OVERCAST, NO SHARING. BUT IF IT'S SUNNY?

SUNNY AND SHARE.

I GOT YOU, BABE.

Depending on your age, you might not know this reference to the pop duo Sonny and Cher. They were very popular in the 1970s and their big hit was "I Got You Babe."

Dear My Girlfriend Pigita,
I recently realized that everyone changes.

But I don't want things to change. I want something good to always be good. And I want the things I count on to always be there to count on.

So I'm now dating a pizza.

WE'LL SEE HOW SHE RESPONDS.

That is at least more durable than a paper envelope.

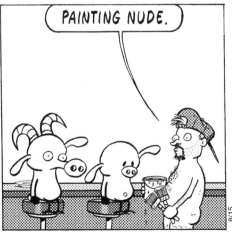

Not quite sure why I felt the need to leave on my hat.

HEY, GOAT, THIS IS MY FRIEND LINDSEY. I THINK YOU MET HER BEFORE.

YEAH, BUT I THINK YOUR HAIR WAS DIFFERENT.

YEAH, I DYE IT, LIKE, EVERY FEW MONTHS.

WHICH MEANS I HAVE TO CHANGE MY PHONE COVER TO MATCH.

PLUS, I'M ALWAYS CHANGING MY SCREEN SAVER. I GET TIRED OF THEM AFTER, LIKE, TWO DAYS.

WHICH REMINDS ME, IT'S PROBABLY TIME FOR ME TO GET MY HAIR DYED AGAIN.

8/16

WELL, THAT'S GREAT.

AND HOW LONG DO THOSE TATTOOS LAST?

MY FAVORITE PART WAS WHEN SHE CALLED YOU 'A SAD OLD MAN WHO'S GONNA DIE SOON.'

IT WAS A FAIR QUESTION.

Strange but true: I generally only put food in the characters' plates or bowls if the food is going to be part of the joke. Otherwise, the plate or bowl is empty.

244

My son Thomas went off to college last year. And I timed these strips to run during the week he was leaving.

It was really tough not having Thomas around, so I texted him all the time. I think I annoyed the bejesus out of him.

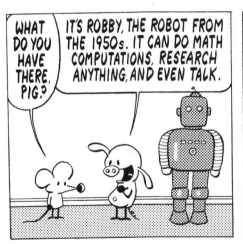

Please do your part by calling that thing a "Stephan Pastis." I want it to be common terminology around the globe.

This was a very popular strip. Apparently, a lot of people have this same problem.

8/23

Norton Hall was the dorm I lived in during my freshman year at the University of California at Berkeley. And 602 was my room. Please feel free to start a shrine at said location.

The *Washington Post* asked me if I would do a drawing to promote their book festival in 2015, as I was one of their featured speakers. I said yes, and gave them this drawing, which I then ran in newspapers as well. So it was sort of a cheap way of getting two uses out of the same drawing. I am nothing if not efficient.

My little love letter to my son.

248

Kids, drug smuggling is a crime. So don't do it, unless you're really, really sure you won't be caught.

[Note from Andrews McMeel Publishing, Stephan's book publisher, regarding the aforementioned comment: Drug smuggling is never okay. Andrews McMeel Publishing does not endorse Stephan's views or comments.]

When you do strips like this, you get e-mails such as this:

Mr. Pastis,
I read your strip today, thought of my husband, and cried. Next time, go for funny, not cruel.

But then you also get e-mails such as this:

Dear Mr. Pastis,
My name is Jayden and I'm a 9-year-old girl in fourth grade. I read your comic three or four times
a week. Today's strip featured neighbor Bill dying in the last panel.

I noticed that his feet were pointed in the wrong direction. If I'm correct, his feet are supposed to be pointed towards
the right. In the fifth panel it looks like he's falling on his back, so his feet should be pointed the other way.

Jayden's e-mail bothered me a lot more than the first one. And not because I got the feet wrong. But because she said she only reads my comic three or four times a week. Please, Jayden, read it every single day.

My knowledge of rap ended in approximately 1985. Thus, my rapper's clothing is about 30 years behind the times.

The word here was "horny," which you cannot say on the comics page.

Is this not logical? Am I the only person who thinks this way?

When *Family Circus* creator Jeff Keane was president of the National Cartoonists Society (a cartooning organization), I prank called him pretending I was a member of the group who was irate over the high cost of the hotel at our annual convention. I kept ripping into Jeff for being a rich cartoonist who could never understand the plight of the common man. After about ten minutes of this (and listening with glee as his frustration grew), I revealed that it was just me.

9/6

This really was how it was when I was a kid. Fortunately, I overcame these obstacles and blossomed into the success I am today.

Bonus Section

(in which all this $#&#
gets even odder)

I've always been impressed by the comic strip *Garfield Minus Garfield*, in which Dan Walsh takes normal *Garfield* strips and erases Garfield from them. The result is truly disturbing, and therefore awesome. If you've never seen it, just go to garfieldminusgarfield.net and read some of them yourself.

So before Dan or some other creative young whippersnapper gets ahold of *Pearls* and does the same thing to my beloved strip, I thought I'd do it to the strip myself. Sort of like the Russians burning down Moscow before Napoleon could get there.

So behold, *Pearls Without Rat*.

Take that, Dan.

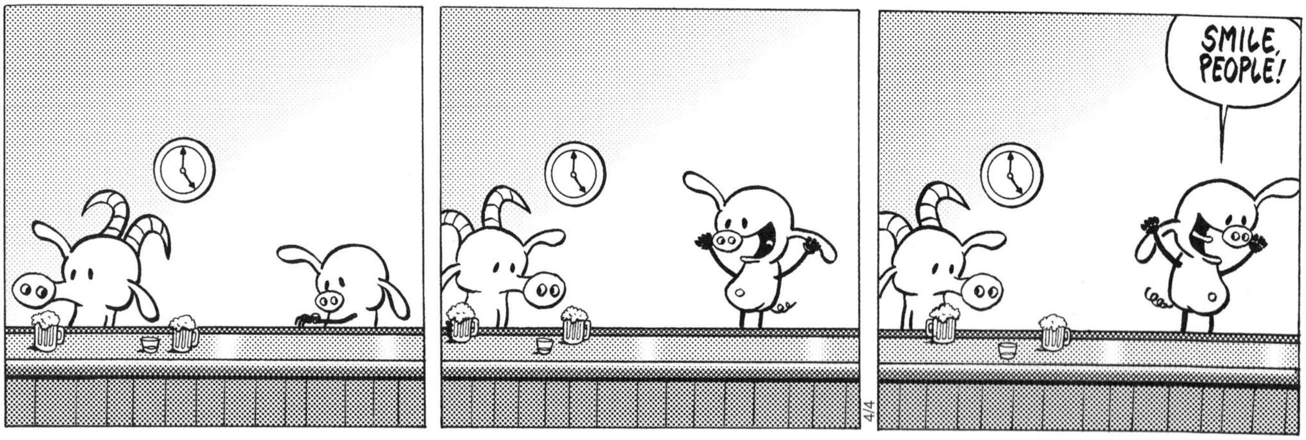
4/4
SMILE, PEOPLE!

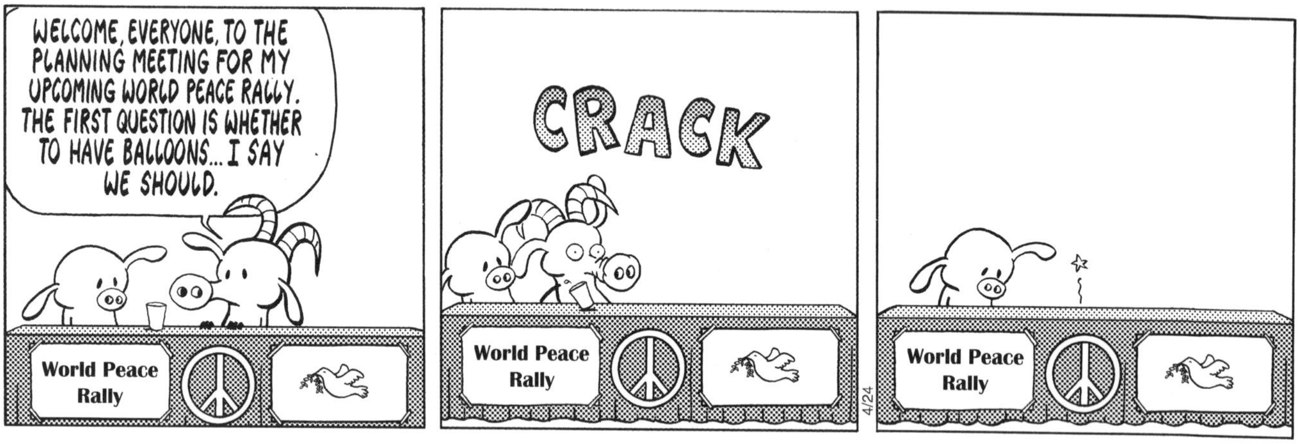
WELCOME, EVERYONE, TO THE PLANNING MEETING FOR MY UPCOMING WORLD PEACE RALLY. THE FIRST QUESTION IS WHETHER TO HAVE BALLOONS... I SAY WE SHOULD.
World Peace Rally
CRACK
World Peace Rally
4/24
World Peace Rally

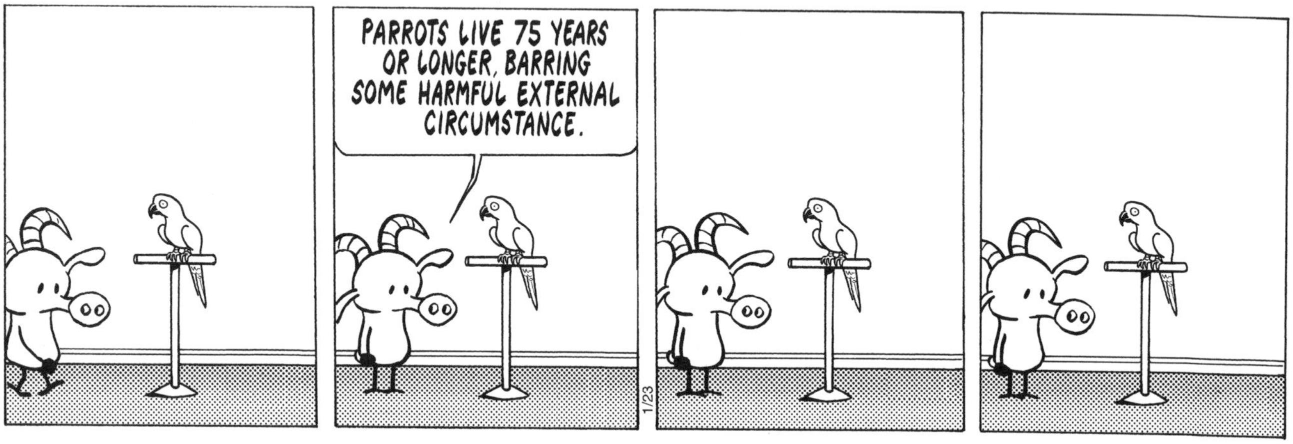
PARROTS LIVE 75 YEARS OR LONGER, BARRING SOME HARMFUL EXTERNAL CIRCUMSTANCE.
1/23

And why only do it with Rat? Let's try *Pearls Without Pig.*

And *Pearls Without Goat.*

And here's a twist. I call it *Pearls Without Speech Balloons.*

And here's one I call *Pearls Without Every Speech Balloon Except for One*.

And another of the same:

And here's another *Pearls Without Every Speech Balloon Except for One*, which oddly enough works better than the original.

And then there's this *Pearls Without Any Speech Balloons at All and Without Pig and Without Rat.*

Which may be the most disturbing of all.

And on that inappropriate note, I say goodbye until the next treasury.

Sincerely,

(INDECIPHERABLE
SIGNATURE)

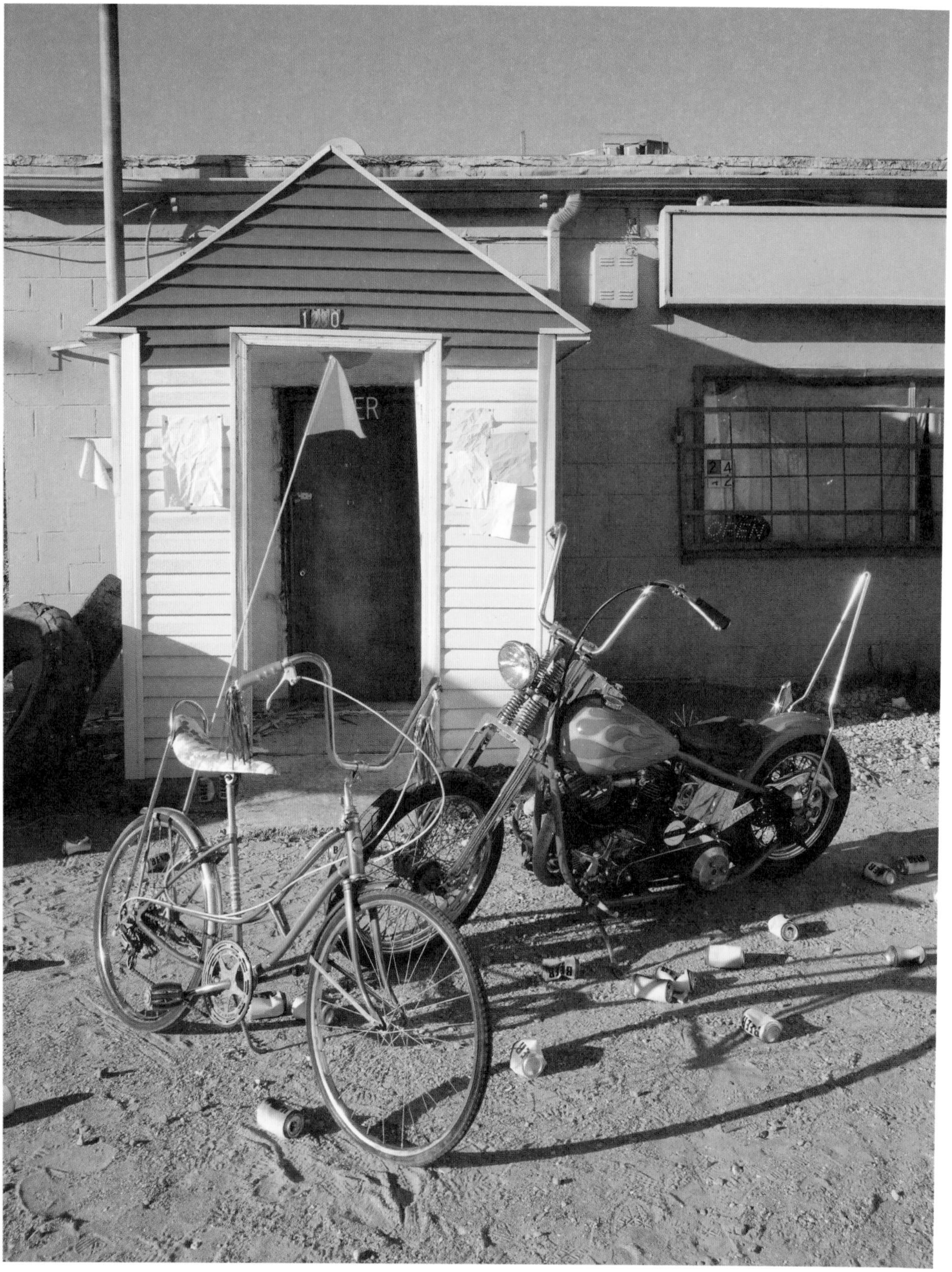
OPEN

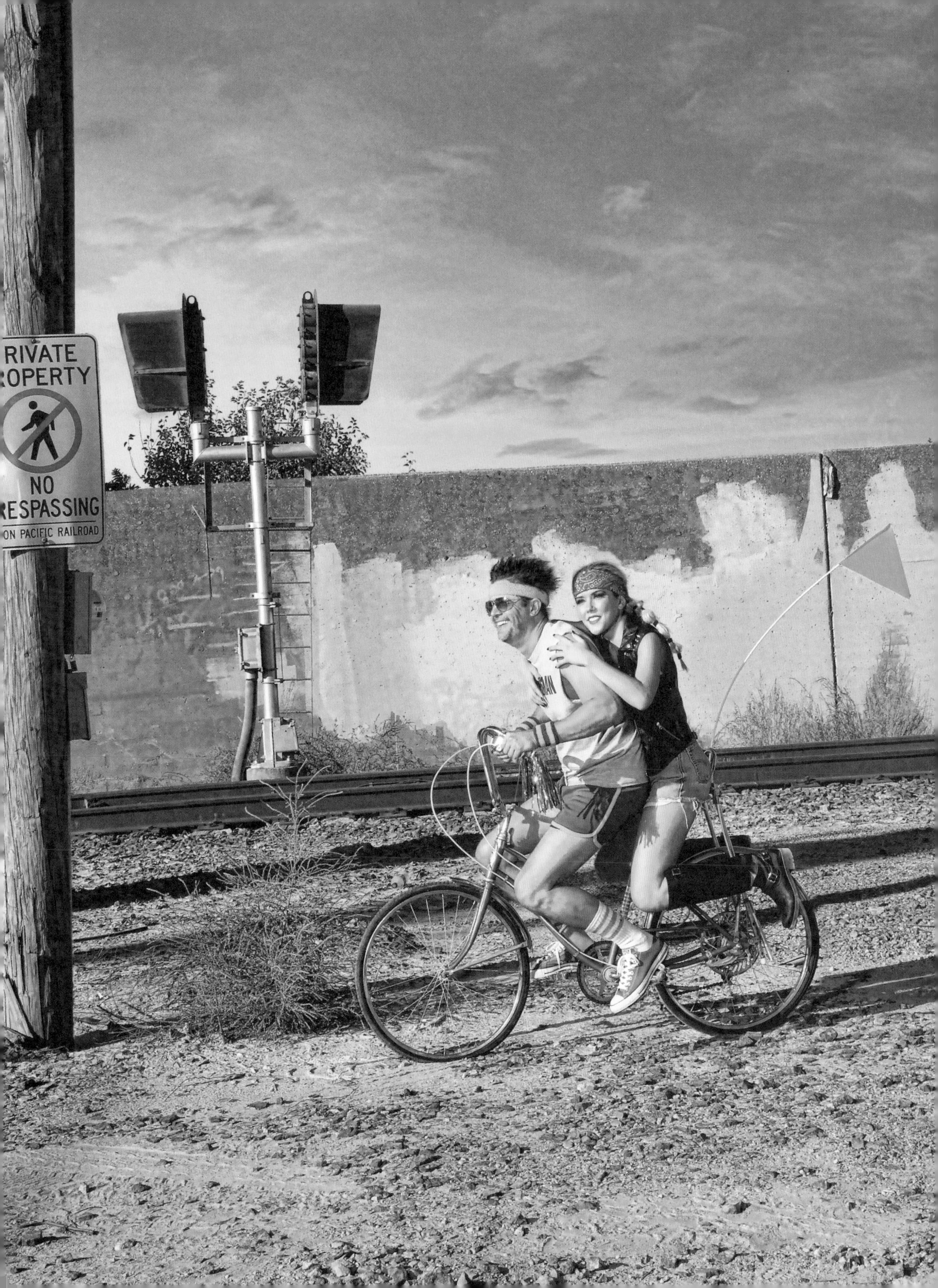
RIVATE
ROPERTY
NO
RESPASSING
ON PACIFIC RAILROAD

Andrews McMeel Publishing
a division of Andrews McMeel Universal
1130 Walnut Street, Kansas City, Missouri 64106

www.andrewsmcmeel.com

17 18 19 20 21 SDB 10 9 8 7 6 5 4 3 2 1

ISBN: 978-1-4494-8366-1

Library of Congress Control Number: 2016951333

Pearls Before Swine can be viewed on the internet at www.pearlscomic.com.

These strips appeared in newspapers from March 3, 2014, to September 6, 2015.

Editor: Dorothy O'Brien
Creative Director: Tim Lynch
Photographer: Thomas Gibson
Text Design: Spencer Williams
Cover Design: Holly Swayne
Production Editor: Grace Bornhoft
Stylist: Andrea Bledsoe

Prop Director: Sher Gibson
Assistants: Thomas Mason and Tony Ontiveros
Image Composite: Graphics Four
Cover Models:
Biker Bar Bouncer: Brian (Bad Ass) Woods
Biker Babe: Kate Dickmann
Chopper: Provided by "Roach"